"For some reason, God doesn't want to change the world without us. Sometimes we are waiting on God, and God is waiting on us. When we ask God to move a mountain, God might give us a shovel. In this book Peter and Alexia remind us that faith has to have feet—the good news needs to become flesh. The gospel is not just about ideas, it's about action; Jesus does not just offer us a presentation of ideas but an invitation to join a movement. As you read *Faith-Rooted Organizing*, keep your eyes open for ways you might be called to become a part of the change we all want to see in the world."

Shane Claiborne, activist and author

"Salvatierra and Heltzel persuasively, provocatively show how organizing can strengthen both Christian churches and the wider communities they are called to serve."

Matthew Myer Boulton, president and professor of theology, Christian Theological Seminary

"As a growing segment of the church reawakens to its calling to 'do justice' in our world, *Faith-Rooted Organizing* will be an indispensable manual for the justice movement. Implementing a beautiful blend of holistic theology, relevant stories and practical wisdom, Alexia and Peter's book clearly illustrates the unique role that Christians have in strategically, prophetically and collaboratively challenging unjust systems and pursuing the common good."

Josh Harper, national director of Urban Projects, InterVarsity Christian Fellowship

"*Faith-Rooted Organizing* will likely become the handbook for those who want to actually *do* faith-based action. Peter and Alexia's firmly grounded scholarship and the important background information given in plain language is simply value added. This book is written by doers for doers. If you wish to make a change, there is no higher praise!"

Randy Woodley, Distinguished Associate Professor of Faith and Culture, Director of Intercultural and Indigenous Studies, George Fox University and Seminary

"By deftly weaving together compelling personal stories, solid theological interpretation and practical organizational expressions, Alexia and Peter have written what could very well become the go-to resource for any leader or organization hoping to faithfully and effectively answer the call to faith-based organizing."

Bruce Reyes-Chow, author of *But I Don't See You as Asian: Curating Conversations About Race*

"Faith-rooted organizing is big on faithfulness, hanging in there, building relationships, training leaders, changing social structures and asking what it means to follow Jesus in today's world. It thus combines the best aspects of resource mobilization theory with what is now ubiquitously called 'framing,' and in this superb book by Alexia Salvatierra and Peter Heltzel, two leading Christian organizers give us a compelling account of what works and what doesn't."

Gary Dorrien, Reinhold Niebuhr Professor of Social Ethics, Union Theological Seminary

"The arts of community organizing have come a long way since the scuffling days of Saul Alinsky and the Back of the Yards organization in Chicago. . . . In writing *Faith-Rooted Organizing* Alexia Salvatierra and Peter Heltzel have made an immense contribution to the maturing of the community organizing tradition in relationship to the mission of the Christian gospel. They begin where people of faith live: in the biblical drama, their local faith communities, their daily walk with Jesus. . . . *Faith-Rooted Organizing* is steeped in real-life experience. Many stories make the concepts come alive. And the book is a love letter from Alexia and Peter to an emerging generation seeking to follow Jesus in lives that matter."

Stephen Paul Bouman, executive director, Congregational and Synodical Mission, Evangelical Lutheran Church in America

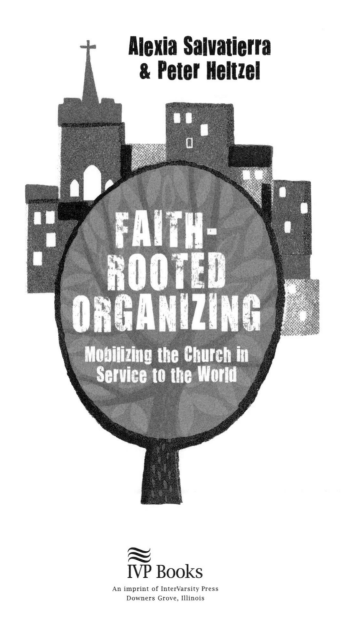

Alexia Salvatierra
& Peter Heltzel

FAITH-ROOTED ORGANIZING

Mobilizing the Church in Service to the World

IVP Books

An imprint of InterVarsity Press
Downers Grove, Illinois

InterVarsity Press
P.O. Box 1400, Downers Grove, IL 60515-1426
ivpress.com
email@ivpress.com

InterVarsity Press® is the book-publishing division of InterVarsity Christian Fellowship/USA®, a movement of students and faculty active on campus at hundreds of universities, colleges and schools of nursing in the United States of America, and a member movement of the International Fellowship of Evangelical Students. For information about local and regional activities, visit intervarsity.org.

All Scripture quotations, unless otherwise indicated, are taken from THE HOLY BIBLE, NEW INTERNATIONAL VERSION®, NIV® Copyright © 1973, 1978, 1984, 2011 by Biblica, Inc.™ Used by permission. All rights reserved worldwide.

While all stories in this book are true, some names and identifying information in this book have been changed to protect the privacy of the individuals involved.

Design: Cindy Kiple
Interior design: Beth Hagenberg
Images: CSA Images/Mod Art Collection/Getty Images

ISBN 978-0-8308-3661-1 (print)
ISBN 978-0-8308-6469-0 (digital)

Printed in the United States of America ∞

Library of Congress Cataloging-in-Publication Data
Salvatierra, Alexia, 1956-
  Faith-rooted organizing : mobilizing the church in service to the world / Rev. Alexia Salvatierra and Dr. Peter Goodwin Heltzel.
      pages cm
  Includes bibliographical references.
  ISBN 978-0-8308-3661-1 (pbk. : alk. paper)
  1. Communities--Religious aspects--Christianity. 2. Community organization. 3. Church work. 4. Evangelistic work. I. Title.
  BV625.S25 2013
  261.8--dc23
                                                                                2013040727

P	18	17	16	15	14	13	12	11	10	9	8	7	6	5	4	3
Y	29	28	27	26	25	24	23	22	21	20	19	18	17	16	15	

Contents

Introduction

Vanessa became a Christian at the beginning of her sophomore year in college. From the moment she experienced the love of Christ, she knew she was called to share that love with her neighbors as effectively as she could, contributing all of the best gifts she could offer. Her passion quickly led her to become a volunteer tutor in an afterschool program in a low-income area.

When she first met thirteen-year-old Rosa, Vanessa was sure that she could minister to her in a way that would be life transforming. Rosa responded to her encouragement, backing away from gang-related friends and beginning to focus on her studies. Vanessa and Rosa began to envision all of the ways Rosa could call upon God's help to give her the strength to make her dreams come true.

What Vanessa did not know was that Rosa, unlike her younger sisters and brothers, was born in another country; she had been brought to the United States without legal permission. Vanessa did not know that Rosa's hard-working mother did not earn enough money to provide rent and food without Rosa's financial help. Vanessa's eagerness and Rosa's fragile new hopes were about to run headlong into barriers that could not be simply solved by determination and faith.

The saying is well known: Give a man a fish and he will eat for a day;

teach him to fish and he will eat for a lifetime. The message is clear that intelligent love goes beyond charity to community development. While it is an act of love to provide a needy person with a hand-out, it is clearly more effective and more empowering to train them for a job, help them to build a house or provide them with after-school tutoring. Learning how to fish is better than receiving fish.

Knowing how to fish, however, is not much use if there is a wall around the fish pond, and fishermen are not allowed access to the water.

Community development strategies reach beyond mere charity to engage people in solving the problems in their neighborhoods. What does not typically get addressed by such strategies are the barriers created by unjust policies, laws and social structures. Community development will not stop air pollution, fix a broken immigration system or ensure the availability of health insurance for workers and their families. Sooner or later, those engaged in community development hit a wall.

Transforming a community requires more than neighborhood development; it demands courageous organizing and persistent strategic advocacy.

Organizing is the practice of bringing people together to create systemic change in their community. Organizing groups may provide direct services and community development to create change, but they also take on the root causes of problems. When they see a wall, they figure out how to take it down.

This kind of effort requires advocacy. *Advocacy* is the process of calling on leaders (whether corporate or governmental) to make public commitments to use their power in ways that respond accurately and effectively to the needs of those affected by their decisions. Through advocacy, public decision-makers end up sharing their decision-making power with their constituents and communities.

Advocacy, in short, makes democracy real. Advocacy is a way for members of a democratic society to exercise the stewardship of influence, utilizing their rights and carrying out their responsibilities. Taken together, organizing and advocacy ensure that fishermen have access to the water, so they can eat for a lifetime, rather than depending on the random act of kindness of someone with an extra fish.

Organizing and Faith: Two Models

In the United States, most organizing models are based on the theories and practice of Saul Alinsky, who began his organizing work in the slums of Chicago in the 1930s. While Alinsky included churches in his organizations, he was primarily focused on neighborhood organizing. Over time, several Alinsky-based organizations developed that focused more centrally on organizing communities of faith, a strategy that is usually called "faith-based organizing."

Faith-based organizers use the same basic assumptions and methodologies that would be employed when organizing any other sector of society, often using faith-oriented principles to articulate the rationale for their methods. While the majority of their organizing is congregational, based in particular faith communities, they involve other community organizations in their networks.[1]

"Faith-rooted organizing," by comparison, goes a step further. Rather than adapting a secular model, faith-rooted organizing is shaped and guided in every way by faith principles and practices. Faith-rooted organizing is based on the belief that many aspects of spirituality, faith traditions, faith practices and faith communities can contribute in unique and powerful ways to the creation of just communities and societies.

Many of the organizing initiatives that have had the greatest impact on society—from the labor initiatives of the early 1900s to the civil rights movement and the Central American Sanctuary Movement—did much more than just incorporate people of faith into Alinsky-style organizing; they drew on the deepest wells of the beliefs, values, disciplines and practices of the people of God.

Faith-rooted organizing is defined and differentiated by faithfully pursuing two questions:

- How can we ensure that our organizing is shaped and guided in all ways by our faith?

- How can we organize people of faith to enable them to contribute all of their unique gifts and resources to the broader movement for justice?

Faith-rooted organizing examines and reevaluates all of the classic components of organizing to explore the potential answers to these questions. It includes and reshapes each of the following core areas of organizing theory and practice:

- Goals: how will the world be different as a result of your organizing?
- Analysis: Where do you start from? What are the obstacles in your path? What resources do you have to address them?
- Strategies: How are you going to move from where you are to where you want to be? What special strategies will the faith community contribute to the movement?
- Recruitment: how will you motivate people to get off their couches, away from their computer and TV screens, and out the front door to join the front line of the struggle for justice in their community?
- Leadership development: how will you equip participants to discern common goals, analyze situations, and develop and implement strategies?
- Sustainability: how will you keep it all going for as long as it takes?

Faith-rooted organizing comprehensively and carefully examines all that faith brings to the table of change—from visions and dreams, to values, to scriptures and sacred texts, to symbols and rituals. Faith-rooted organizing recognizes all of the particular gifts and resources not only of individuals with faith but of the holistic spiritual communities where faith is nurtured and expressed. It is not designed to denigrate or replace other forms of organizing. It assumes a fully multisector, broad-based movement for justice, functioning like a body in which each part does what it does best. Faith-rooted organizing is designed to enable the faith "sector" to give its best to the whole.

The vision for faith-rooted organizing comes from the concrete experience of global justice movements such as the multisectoral movement in the Philippines formed against the dictator Ferdinand Marcos and his historic exploitation of the poor, and Central American movements to end the ownership and control of land by a few families to achieve full democracy.

In these movements, individuals were seen to be active in a variety of sectors over the course of their lifetimes but continued to participate in an overall movement toward a better world. A collective understanding of human nature and identity led them to believe that each sector (students, workers, faith leaders, mothers, etc.) has specific gifts to offer and can best offer those gifts when they are organized in a way that is tailored to their context. The various sectors then learn from and inspire one another.

This approach has transferred well from the Philippines and Latin America to other contexts. Altagracia Perez, an Episcopalian priest and leader in a faith/community/labor coalition in Los Angeles, notes that when faith and labor worked collaboratively while each maintaining their own separate identity and organizing approaches, each was pushed by the other to live up to its highest values.

Faith-rooted organizing is a model built on a foundation of international strategies of system disruption and transformation for the good of the least among us and the common good. Its structure has been developed (informally) by faith-inspired leaders such as Mahatma Gandhi, Martin Luther King Jr., Oscar Romero, Gustavo Gutierrez and Cesar Chavez—all of whom, in their own ways, were motivated by the way of Jesus.[2] The model also builds on the theology, theory and practices of many lesser known leaders in the U.S. civil rights movement and the Central American Sanctuary Movement. As a coherent model, however, faith-rooted organizing is new, developed in the twenty-first century and tested by the work of young religious leaders in Clergy and Laity United for Economic Justice (CLUE).

CLUE-CA is a grassroots alliance of California faith leaders from all religious traditions who join low-wage workers in their struggles for a living wage, health insurance, fair working conditions and a voice in the economic decisions that affect their lives. CLUE-CA also works at removing barriers that keep low-wage workers from full participation in the workplace and the community—barriers such as a broken immigration policy and dysfunctional criminal justice systems. CLUE-LA is a Los Angeles chapter where much of what became the faith-rooted organizing model was worked out.

Because faith-rooted organizing is so centered in Scripture, theology and spirituality, faith communities with little prior involvement in organizing and advocacy find it to be a good on-ramp to such efforts, thereby contributing their unique resources and gifts to larger collaborative initiatives for social justice. It is designed as a twenty-first century open source model—a phrase borrowed from the world of computer technology which assumes that any approach to solving a problem is improved by the free and ongoing integration of best practices from other approaches. The concepts and training exercises of faith-rooted organizing are meant to be available to anyone who wants to bring people of faith together to create comprehensive change.

Faith-rooted organizing is not a model in the traditional sense. It is a toolbox, an orientation and a way of life. Faith-rooted organizing is never a finished product; it is designed to encourage sharing of best practices wherever and whenever they occur. In alignment with this philosophy, this book will incorporate the theological insights of an international network of faith-oriented justice scholars, exploring the implications of their insights on the ground. It will also include quotes from faith-rooted activists involved in the great movements of the twentieth century, as well as stories from various places around the country where faith-rooted organizing is currently being practiced.[3] This is a book written by community for community.

In connection with this innovative approach of community-to-community teaching, we are each writing in our own voices, in dialogue with each other. A quick introduction to us:

Alexia is a Lutheran pastor with over thirty years of experience in organizing and ministry. The faith-rooted organizing model was developed under her leadership as the executive director of CLUE-LA and CLUE California for eleven years. She now teaches the model in various forms around the world, consulting for ministries and organizations such as World Vision, InterVarsity Christian Fellowship, the Christian Community Development Association and a variety of denominations, and teaching as adjunct faculty for various Christian colleges and seminaries. Alexia was inspired to write this book by two young women she wants to pass the torch to: Alina Consuelo Ortiz Salvatierra (her daughter) and Kim Yehsong (a young campus ministry leader in Chicago). You are invited to listen in as she shares the core of her message with them at the end of each chapter.

Peter is a theologian, pastor and activist in New York City. He teaches theology at New York Theological Seminary where he directs the Micah Institute. Inspired by the prophet Micah's call to do justice, love mercy and walk humbly with God (Micah 6:8), the Micah Institute educates faith leaders to fight poverty and injustice. The Micah Institute has played an important role in organizing clergy for a new living wage movement through a growing multicultural faith/community/labor coalition in New York City. Peter lives out the depths of his theological training on the streets of the city as a pastor at Park Avenue Christian Church.

This book is designed to introduce you to the principles and practices of faith-rooted organizing being used by prophetic evangelical Christians around the United States. It will provide a theological and scriptural foundation that clarifies God's call to engage in faith-rooted organizing. Throughout this book we will intertwine the testimonies of a cloud of witnesses into our presentation of this model. We welcome you to the adventure![4]

1

The Roots of Faith-Rooted Organizing

The history of justice movements around the world has much to teach us. If we seek to change our communities for the better, we will find ourselves standing on the shoulders of generations of activists and organizers.

Unfortunately, as traditionally practiced, community organizing—the effort at bringing a community together to fight for its rights and improve its situation—neglects history, focusing instead on the present and the future.

By contrast, faith is profoundly historical. The God of the Bible acts in and through history. Our salvation occurs in the context of a long history of redemption. Christian mystics, rooted in a personal relationship with God, are aflame in their prophetic witness in and for the world.

In fact, many of the most significant leaders of the great movements for justice of the twentieth century were people of great faith. In the civil rights movement led by Martin Luther King Jr., in movements for justice in Central America, in the Central American Sanctuary Movement in the United States and in the farm workers movement led by Cesar Chavez— we find faith at the heart and the root of each effort. In this chapter we'll explore the mystical-prophetic underpinnings of the great organizing movements of the twentieth century, with an eye toward how their experience might inform our efforts today.

Shalom Justice

The black freedom struggle that led to the American civil rights movement was animated by a marriage of mysticism and prophetic witness.[1] While mystical union with God is often constructed as individual union with God in Christ, it is better understood as having a communal context: covenantal participation in God mediated through active participation in the church. Mystical experience is rooted in personal relationship with the Living God, but it always engages the community. The glory of God is thus revealed in what is often called *shalom justice*.

The prophetic witness of such movements recalls the love and justice of God and the prophetic imperative in the Old Testament based on God's justice and righteousness. Transliterated from Hebrew as *mishpat* and *sadiqah*, justice and righteousness are brought together in prophetic discourse time and again, reminding Israel of its mission to restore creation's shalom as a concrete way of worshiping the Creator. As Nicholas Wolterstorff writes:

> God desires that each and every human being shall flourish . . . and experience what the Old Testament writers call shalom. Injustice is perforce the impairment of shalom. That is why God loves justice. God desires the flourishing of each and every one of God's human creatures; justice is indispensable to that. Love and justice are not pitted against each other but are intertwined.[2]

Wolterstorff helps us to see that the struggle for justice must be rooted in the mystical and prophetic streams of Christianity.

The burning bush of Moses comes to mind because it illustrates the deep connectedness between the mystical and the prophetic. Moses learns two things in this divine encounter: God's most personal and precious name, and God's most earnest message of liberation for the oppressed. In this way Moses' encounter with God is both mystical and prophetic, and he is radically transformed: from royal felon in flight to spokesman for the liberation of the Hebrew people, from one avoiding politics at all cost to one who stands face to face with Pharaoh.

Central to both the prophetic and the mystical is love. Through love, we open ourselves to receive the hidden things of God, mysterious knowing that is dark and inarticulate but at once and the same time arresting and illuminating. Through this experience, we learn that God's love is always turned outward, oriented toward the poor. Our love becomes organized by this mystical rootedness to love the other, the poor and weak. Soon, we are aflame with God's love for justice amidst all peoples. Central to living shalom, then, was loving the Lord "with all your heart and with all your soul and with all your strength" (Deuteronomy 6:4) and also caring for the marginalized—widows, orphans, strangers and the poor (Zechariah 7:9-10).

The prophetic call to shalom justice in the Hebrew Bible converges in the person of Jesus Christ. Jesus of Nazareth in his person embodies God's love and justice for the world. His teaching of the kingdom of God unveils the pretense of imperial power and offers the countours of a new order of love and justice. As a Jewish improvisor on Torah, Jesus presses the tradition to a radically inclusive love; when he heals a man on the sabbath, for example (see Mark 3:1-6; Luke 13:10-17), he improvises with the law toward the end of loving restoration. Love is, therefore, the avoidance of any act of violence or dominance over another. When we read through Paul's famous summation of love we find no act of dominion, for that always necessitates an act of violence. Love, says Paul, "is patient, love is kind. . . . It always protects, always trusts, always hopes, always perseveres" (1 Corinthians 13:4-7).

In the work of Martin Luther King Jr. and Cesar Chavez we see a mystical and prophetic commitment to both patience and kindness. They did not capitulate to the powers that be, for that is not prophetic. They stood their ground calling for an end to oppression. But neither did they capitulate to the vilification of their opponents, for that would be a rejection of the mystical work of love inspired in them by God. As we will see, their faith would give a unique quality to their efforts, with a unique force to their results.

Martin Luther King Jr. and the Civil Rights Movement

For Martin Luther King Jr., the goal of the civil rights movement was beloved community—the place where everyone is recognized as being equally and infinitely precious, where everyone is welcomed, valued and respected.[3] Every institution in the United States had been set up, unconsciously or consciously, to legitimate and perpetuate white male power and privilege. Christians were at the center of movements of resistance to this racial injustice: Sojourner Truth and Harriet Tubman worked to abolish slavery; Ida B. Wells fought to end lynching; Fanny Lou Hamer and Ella Baker fought for the civil rights movement. King saw the establishment of beloved community on earth as a translation of Jesus' teaching of the kingdom of God. Thus, King's contribution to America's political future was first and foremost theological.

For King, God created all people in the divine image (*imago Dei*) and the universe is founded on God's justice.[4] Every person is sacred, unique, dignified and loved by God, and thus must be fully and meaningfully incorporated into the human community. The church is called to embody the boundless love of God by being a community of radical welcome to all God's children.

King's vision was inspired by Jesus' teaching, which had a dynamic "already" and "not yet" character.[5] For King, "beloved community" refers to the "already," earthly manifestation of the kingdom of God—the "creation of a society where all men can live together as brothers, where every man will respect the dignity and the worth of human personality."[6] For King the civil rights movement made possible not only the liberation of individual African Americans but also a new social order: "The end is reconciliation, the end is redemption, the end is the creation of beloved community."[7]

While King's vision of beloved community developed gradually, he had a dramatic conversion to faith-rooted organizing. The night his home in Montgomery was bombed, King prayed at his kitchen table for God's help. In the stillness of that moment King resolved to continue the quest for justice and the development of the beloved community. His heart was enflamed with love for God as a motivation for the movement for justice. King became inspired by multicolored dreams of democracy, a dream he was dedicated to making a reality. As historian Troy Jackson writes,

King's optimistic, hope-filled message rooted in the power of God inspired men and women to remain in and sacrifice for the struggle. His consistent emphasis on the love ethic found in the life and teachings of Jesus provided the theological undergirding for the strategy of nonviolence. King's growing faith in God also fueled his conviction that the civil rights movement could become a vehicle for redemption in Montgomery, the South and the throughout the whole nation.[8]

King's legendary 1963 speech "I Have a Dream" is one of the most memorable expressions of his vision of beloved community. A synthesis of Jesus' ideal of the kingdom of God and the American dream, King proclaimed his dream to be "deeply rooted in the American dream that one day this nation will rise up and live out the true meaning of its creed—we hold these truths to be self-evident, that all men are created equal." The dream is inclusive of all people—"black men and white men, Jews and Gentiles, Catholics and Protestants."[9] Drawing liberally from the deep river of the black church tradition, King's call was nevertheless to every U.S. citizen: one day all people, regardless of race, creed or color, can sit down together, learn together, play together, serve together. In so doing King provides not only an image of the beloved community but also a concrete embodiment of it (Jesus Christ) as well as a political process toward achieving it—nonviolent love.

Toward the end of King's life, he began to expand his focus from racial segregation in the United States to human rights throughout the world.[10] In his sermon "A Time to Break Silence," delivered on April 4, 1967, at New York's Riverside Church, King argued that the American empire was "the greatest purveyor of violence in the world today."[11] Racism, materialism and militarism were all based on a logic of violence; they could only be permanently dismantled through nonviolent love. So King proposed to dismantle the "powers and principalities" of racism, poverty and war by building a large-scale, nonviolent coalition for justice.

The poor remained King's ultimate focus, a conviction rooted in Jesus' teaching of the kingdom as good news to the poor (Luke 4:18-19; 7:22).

Jesus' parables communicate his vision of the just and peaceable kingdom.[12] His miracles, healings and solidarity with the poor, outsiders and victims served as a living demonstration of shalom justice.[13] Even his Spirit-empowered cruciform life was a parable of the kingdom, offering clues about the shape of the just and peaceable kingdom. Scattering mustard seeds of hope throughout Galilee, Jesus' kingdom grew quickly, offering life-giving love to individuals, communities and the land.[14]

King and others saw this aspect of the gospel clearly, and so the U.S. civil rights movement could be described as a provisional expression of the just and peaceable kingdom of God. King laid out a theological drama in which a reconciled humanity was central both to the means and ends of the movement.[15]

Faith-Rooted Visions of Justice in Latin America

The wave of revolution against the established order that characterized the 1960s in the United States also occurred internationally. Throughout the world, movements for justice were gaining momentum and resulting in rapid social change.

In Latin America, faith leaders played a significant role in advocating for justice for the poor. Their efforts were shaped by their theology which in turn was formed by their interpretation of the core messages of Scripture. While these pastors and teachers differed in many respects, their common insight was that biblical interpretation has often been influenced by social perspective and economic location. The wealthiest nations, as well as the richest individuals, bring a different set of lenses to their reading of Scripture than the poor; historically they have had the social power to assert that their interpretations are correct and, furthermore, to limit access to other interpretations.

In Bible studies with poor *campesinos* throughout Latin America, Catholic leaders like Gustavo Gutierrez and Protestant leaders like Jose Miguez Bonino and Medardo Gomez (of the Lutheran Church of El Salvador) sought to place the Bible directly into the hands of the poor— people who most needed to hear all of the ways in which the gospel is meant to be good news. Although they were often maligned as "communists" who "politicized" the Bible, their goal was simply to build a "theology of the people" that spoke God's love into the real circumstances of extreme injustice that had existed in Latin America for centuries.

In *The Gospel in Solentiname*, a transcript of Bible studies with Nicaraguan peasants compiled by Ernesto Cardinal, Olivia (a campesina mother) read the Gospel of Luke for herself for the first time:

> I remember the priests used to preach to us that the Protestants were blind guides. But they themselves were on the side of the rich and the powerful. They were really the blind guides. Catholics or Protestants, blind guides are the ones who read the Gospel that says, "Woe to you rich!" and they're so comfortable they don't see it. They preached a lot of things, but they didn't preach love, and they didn't practice. And we were blind in that same chain and we didn't show any love for others either.[16]

At the same time, several evangelical leaders in Latin America also began to reflect on the Biblical call to justice. Rene Padilla and Samuel Escobar coined the term *mision integral* ("holistic mission") to talk about discipleship that integrated spirituality, evangelism and social justice. Justo Gonzalez, a Methodist theologian, published Bible Study guides for local churches that lifted up justice themes.

The first fruit of this theological awakening was inspiration and sustaining strength for those who sought justice. As the numbers of faith leaders grew and their commitment increased correspondingly, the repressive regimes of Latin America responded with waves of retaliation and repression. Archbishop Oscar Romero, a well-known advocate for justice in El Salvador, was assassinated while he was celebrating Holy Communion in 1980. In the months before his murder, catechists in El Salvador who carried Bibles publicly reported being routinely harassed and often severely beaten by soldiers who saw them as "communists." Many told stories of friends and family who had "disappeared" because of their widely known commitment to justice for the poor.

While many pastors and congregational leaders in Central America became martyrs, many others became refugees. In the decade from 1980 to 1990, roughly 500,000 Central Americans came to the United States fleeing civil wars in Central America. At the time, U.S. asylum policy employed a different set of standards for individuals from hostile countries than for U.S. allies, and the U.S. government had been funding Central American dictatorships for many years. At the same time that human rights organizations were documenting widespread atrocities in Guatemala, for example, only 5 percent of Guatemalans who applied for political asylum were approved. When Christian congregational leaders discovered that they could not obtain political asylum in the United States, they asked for "sanctuary" in the churches.

Sanctuary is a term drawn from the biblical concept of the cities of refuge. In Numbers 35, the people of Israel are given an institutional remedy for situations where a lawbreaker is likely to receive unjustly cruel punishment. "Cities of refuge" are set apart as sites of sanctuary for individuals who have committed manslaughter but are being treated as if they have committed murder. The people of God are to protect the lawbreakers until they can get a fair hearing and a just punishment for their crime. This biblical tradition has resulted in laws all across the globe protecting the right of faith communities to offer protection to lawbreakers who fit into this category.

The United States has never formally provided this right to churches, although U.S. Christians have often assumed the role. In the 1980s, Presbyterian pastor John Fife and Quaker philosopher John Corbett began a Central American Sanctuary Movement which at its height saw hundreds of congregations across the country providing sanctuary to Central American refugees. Ultimately, the movement succeeded in reforming the legislation governing political asylum; a uniform set of humanitarian criteria was developed and kept independent of political alliances.

The Sanctuary Movement depended on strategies that were markedly different from those used by traditional community organizers—most notably in that the U.S. citizens who protected Central Americans at the risk of arrest and prosecution were not motivated by self-interest. Rather, they described themselves as moved by faith and solidarity.

This passionate self-sacrifice for the wellbeing of others, often expressly in the name and spirit of Jesus Christ, commanded the respect of the broader society and the attention of the political leadership. They won the trust of the average American precisely because of the moral authority that came from their willingness to sacrifice for the truth. They echoed the new theology of the Latin American Christians who were arriving at the doors of their churches as refugees—prioritizing, in word and deed, the needs and perspective of the poor in the pursuit of the common good.

Cesar Chavez and the Farmworkers

Cesar Chavez (1927-1993) was a Mexican American labor organizer. Trained in the techniques of Saul Alinsky, he cofounded the National Farm Workers Association. A mystically rooted Christian, Chavez often used biblical narratives and papal writings in his organizing efforts. He was mentored by labor-activist priest Donald McDonnell and sought to embody the imitation of Christ in both his personal life and his social activism. Chavez transformed traditional organizing through a deep theological and moral understanding of labor from his heritage in the Catholic Church.[17]

When Chavez began organizing farm workers, they were being kept in an impoverished and powerless state by the well-organized and powerful lobbying of commercial farm owners. Commercial farm lobbying efforts had been successful in keeping agricultural workers from being covered by the National Labor Relations Board Act. This exclusion meant that no labor standards, including health and safety, would apply to agricultural workers. Furthermore, farm workers had little to no job security. As part of an unstructured workforce, farm workers could easily be fired for any attempt to organize. Owners of these farms encouraged the government to maintain a continual supply of migrant labor flowing in from impoverished provinces of Mexico so that any employee could be easily replaced.

Chavez's personal faith and commitment to costly discipleship led him to organize faith leaders to resist these unjust conditions. The National Farmworker Ministry, an ecumenical Protestant organization traditionally dedicated to providing charity to impoverished farmworker families, was one of Chavez's earliest and most dedicated allies. And then, when he began the 1965-1970 Delano Grape Strike and Boycott, he appealed to the National Conference of Catholic Bishops for support.

After their own internal communications, Catholic Bishops intervened in the Delano Grape Strike and Boycott to act as mediators between grape growers and the United Farm Workers Organizing Committee. This intervention fostered trust and reached a culminating point in April 1970, when Lionel Steinberg, owner of the largest table-grape farm in Coachella Valley, "signed a contract with Chavez in a widely-publicized ceremony at the chancery of the Los Angeles archdiocese."[18] This set in place a model for honest brokering for union contracts. Bishops continued to be invited to act as observers in subsequent contract negotiations, ensuring that both parties—workers and growers—were negotiating in good faith.

Roman Catholic ritualism, with its deep symbolism and ancient traditions, inspired the most well-known faith-rooted action by California farm workers: the pilgrimage from Delano to Sacramento. Lifting a cross intertwined with grape leaves, Chavez walked not only to publicize the plight of California farm workers but to also build solidarity among those workers and draw in potential allies to the cause of labor justice. On Easter Day 1966, ten thousand pilgrims converged in Sacramento, California's state capitol.

Chavez also called upon his religious tradition for an internal organizing strategy. The extended duration of a major strike caused a mutiny in which key farm worker leaders advocated for the abandonment of the principles and practices of non-violence. Instead of organizing a meeting to discuss the problem, or even meeting individually with key leaders, Chavez embarked on a lengthy fast. Farm workers from throughout the union came to join him in fasting and praying. His critics lost the ability to sway significant numbers of the union members and were forced to concede.

Chavez's faith-rooted nonviolent strategies had real-world power to change hearts, most memorably in his confrontation with Hollis Roberts, owner of properties where peaches, plums and grapes were grown. Roberts had a reputation as a stalwart and unwavering believer in the free market. He was initially hostile to organized labor and especially to Chavez, labeling him a communist. When Roberts finally decided to negotiate with the United Farm Workers, he claimed that his shift was not merely a result of the economic pressure caused by the strike but more so that he'd come to recognize the error of his own perception and attitude toward the rights of workers in his fields. "I learned that I was wrong," he reported. "I learned that Cesar Chavez is not a communist, that he is a God-fearing, Christian gentleman."[19]

       • • •

Dear Alina and Yehsong:

Dr. King and the other leaders of the civil rights movement, the great teachers of liberation theology, the leaders of the Sanctuary Movement, Cesar Chavez and the farmworkers are part of the great cloud of witnesses that surround you. Listen to them and learn from them; their faith was at the core of their organizing and they laid a foundation for the practice of faith-rooted organizing.

Also, note how the story of their lives and work is a parable of the kingdom of God as well as a poignantly human tale. Their accomplishments are marvelous and more than they could have done without the power of the Spirit behind, in and through them.

But, as Jesus said, "you will do greater works than these" (John 14:12).

2

Dreaming God's Dream Together

The Goals of Faith-Rooted Organizing

If organizing is bringing people together to create change, then in order to organize effectively, you have to know what kind of change you want to create. You need to have a clear picture of the intended product of your organizing. You need to know how the world will be different when your work is done. As the saying (often attributed to Jesse Jackson Sr.) goes, "If you don't know where you are going, you can't get there."

In short, you need goals—both ultimate goals and interim goals. You need benchmarks that indicate that the work is being achieved.

By definition, the goals of organizing include changes that individuals cannot achieve on their own. Organizing seeks to create systemic community change. However, different organizing approaches have distinct ways of understanding the nature of the change that they seek and the goals that embody it. To understand the unique contribution of faith-rooted organizing to the goal-setting process, we have to begin with two interconnected stories.

Dreams and Visions

In the early 1990s, the prolonged civil wars in Central America ended. Former Costa Rican president and Nobel Peace Prize winner Oscar Arias played an important role in this process through a behind-the-scenes, informal peace process in El Salvador and Guatemala. Until President Arias carried out his Roundtables for Peace, the formal peace processes facilitated by the United Nations had been unsuccessful. The agreements achieved by Arias formed the basis for the final peace accords.

I (Alexia) was young at the time, working for Vesper Society, a Lutheran non-profit which was committed to international peace. Vesper was a sponsor of the roundtables and was given an observer seat at the table; as one of the very few employees who spoke fluent Spanish, I was allowed to represent the organization. The experience was life-changing.

In both El Salvador and Guatemala, Arias invited top leaders of all the major sectors of society to attend a closed conversation. CEOs of major corporations, union presidents, the archbishop, the university presidents and the directors of human rights organizations (as well as rebel leaders and generals) were included. The atmosphere in the beginning was tense; some of the participants had been directly or indirectly responsible for the deaths of one another's relatives. President Arias started the first session by asking each participant to write down on an index card their personal dreams and their dreams for their country. Each participant went to the front of the room, talked about their dreams and taped their card to the wall.

As the exercise went on, it became clear to all that their dreams for their country were essentially the same. Everyone wanted prosperity; everyone wanted the peace that is required to produce and sustain it. The atmosphere in the room changed and dialogue became possible. The potential for the future became more important than the pain of the past. In Guatemala, the formal peace accords were signed one week after the Roundtable concluded; they incorporated the points of agreement reached at the Roundtable.

In 2009, CLUE used a similar exercise with a group of congregational leaders in South Los Angeles. Those gathered represented primarily African American and immigrant congregations in a place in which the conflict between these groups has been terrible and often violent. Dreams were expressed in different languages, but the content was the same: everyone wanted safe housing, good schools, living wage jobs and neighborhood unity.

It was clear, however, that the exercise initially had less impact in South Los Angeles than in Central America. As the group struggled together, the trainers realized that the weakness of the exercise came from the lack of confidence that their common dreams could come true. This character- istic is shared by many residents of poor communities.

The trainers responded by adding a component. After creating the dream wall, the group was asked to reflect on God's dreams for their com- munity. When they realized how much God supports their common dreams, a surprised and delighted laughter spread through the room. At this moment, participants shared the same experience of unity through a common dream with the Central American leaders, as well as shared hope that they would be able to make their dreams real together.

In faith-rooted organizing, we believe we can answer the question, "How do we want the world to be different because of our efforts?" by casting a common vision rooted in God's vision. This is not a typical or traditional way to determine the goals of an organizing process. By looking at other ways that organizing sets goals, we'll arrive at a more in-depth description of the faith-rooted approach.

Issue-Based Goals

Before Saul Alinsky's contribution to the field of community organizing (and still today, to a lesser extent), U.S. groups working on community change tended to focus on very specific social problems. For example, an organization is created to work specifically on affordable housing or en- vironmental protection. The organization has goals that are practical and concrete; for example, to create a housing fund or to reduce pollution by corporations. Their work is focused on the most direct approach to solving the problem, which is often the attainment of a specific public policy change. There are various weaknesses to this approach if the primary goal is the creation of lasting and comprehensive change.

First, people who join such an organization tend to be only those who care about its specific concern. Each organization focuses on a different concern, inciting competition for the same resources, volunteers and power. These divisions weaken each organization's capacity to achieve meaningful and lasting social change.

Second, the commitment to an issue-based campaign naturally ebbs and flows. When the organization wins a significant policy victory, participants tend to feel like they have done their job. Many volunteer leaders and organization members turn their attention to other interests. The fate of the issue is left in the hands of policymakers who may not share the perspectives or commitments of the organization. Without shifting the balance of power in society, policy victories are fragile, easily lost when sympathetic institutional policymakers leave their position or the pressure on indifferent or unsympathetic policymakers ebbs.

The Goal of Building Power

Saul Alinsky was a robust critic of issue-based organizing. One of his most important insights was that the weaknesses of goal-based organizing could be overcome if organizing efforts set goals beyond single issues. His strategy was to build power for broader community change.

Alinsky suggested that the core purpose of organizing was to build power: "We are concerned with how to create mass organizations to seize power and give it to the people."[1] While Alinsky-based organizing does set policy goals (extracting them from the solutions that community members propose to resolve their common problems), its fundamental effort is to build the power of the whole community.

When the members of a community create change in a way that develops civic participation skills, ongoing bonds of relationship and a commitment to exercise voice and power, the forward momentum and unified force necessary for lasting change is created. This force can then be used to deal with a wide variety of social issues. In this way, an organization which intentionally builds power for its members can achieve and maintain far more than organizations focused primarily on solving a specific problem.

Alinsky's approach, however, assumes that giving a particular community power will result in the best use of that power. The Christian doctrine of sin throws this assumption into question. Sin, in the form of the human attraction to deny others human dignity and seek power for selfish ambition, is a perennial problem. Sin also has an institutional dimension when the institutions of society, like banks, schools, and governments, become oppressive "powers and principalities" that must be prophetically confronted.[2] While faith-rooted organizing shares Alinsky's goal of unleashing the power of the community, it also acknowledges the tendency for human beings to abuse power and for institutions to be sites of systemic oppression. This is a more realistic assessment of human institutions. Neither the rich nor the poor can escape this innate temptation to oppress others.

Faith-rooted organizing contends that our sinful tendencies can be partially contained and corrected by the guidance of the Word of God. The values and visions in Scripture challenge us to question our self-serving assumptions and impulses. Racism and other critical, systematic sins are to be confronted by faith-rooted organizers.

The Problem of Self-Interest

While Alinsky sought to help common laborers in their struggle for economic justice, he did not initially acknowledge the importance of race and ethnicity. For example, his first famous community organization, "The Back of the Yards," excluded African American residents in a variety of ways. As Jeffrey Stout notes:

> Alinsky became increasingly worried by what happened to the Back of the Yards community after his organizing efforts bore fruit. Poor whites, most of them Polish-Catholic immigrants, used the power generated by their community organization to improve their economic and political standing in the arena of Chicago politics. As they became middle class and established their foothold in the Chicago political machine, they eventually used their power against other relatively disempowered communities.[3]

The racial struggle in Chicago illustrates a fundamental flaw in Alinsky's method: there is no built-in requirement that the organized community consider any danger in the desire for power. While the Polish in Back of the Yards were marginalized as an immigrant group, they were also over time racialized as "white."[4] Thus, they had more power and privilege than their African American neighbors. Alinsky was forced to confront the reality of white supremacy through the pushback to his organizing efforts.

Alinsky was an optimist, believing that "if people have the power to act, in the long run they will, most of the time, reach the right decisions."[5] But "most of the time" is not all the time. Sometimes the people make a bad decision. And since racism is a perennial problem in the United States, antiracist analysis becomes critical to ensuring that wise decisions are made in the work of organizing. Modern Alinsky-based organizing has responded to the problem of racial difference and the struggle for universal values by attempting to define the communities engaged in the organization in broader terms. "Broad-based" organizing tries to link communities with different ethnic and geographic identities in a common search for power. However, the complexities involved in spreading power across a broader base are evident.

Meanwhile, the academy is beginning to take note of the power of community organizing. Philosopher and democratic theorist Jeffrey Stout's *Blessed Are the Organized: Grassroots Democracy in America,* one of the most important books in religious ethics in thirty years, affirms that community organizing was the driver of social movements such as the civil rights movement and the women's movement. He uses Alinsky as his model, however, and so Stout's vision suffers from many of the problems of the Alinsky legacy. While he is correct that there exists "the dependence of the ruling elites on the deference of ordinary people,"[6] and that the "sleepers" must rise up not one by one but as a communal force, faith-rooted organizers maintain that it is not simply self-interest that awakens the sleepers, but a deep commitment to the prophetic scriptural traditions. As Christians, while we may value democracy, we cannot imbue it with a completely blind faith, nor can we ignore the biblical command to take care of our neighbor.

Faith not only sees the immanent dynamics of power, but it is open to interruption, the inbreaking reality of that which is not simply more of the same but a new reality. It resists treating people instrumentally, which is part and parcel of a worldview like Alinsky's that is governed by instrumental reason.

Faith-rooted organizing aspires beyond democracy to establish the beloved community. Our colleagues in organized struggle are not instruments; we make revolutionary friendships for the long haul. For faith-rooted organizers, the love of God and the hope of the beloved community wake us up to work on behalf of the marginalized and the oppressed.

Some networks that were originally Alinsky-based have moved significantly beyond Alinsky's understanding of the goal of building power. Over the past decade the Pacific Institute for Community Organizing (PICO) has been reimagining the concepts of Alinsky, launching a national Prophetic Voices initiative to call on clergy, faith leaders and congregations to bring biblically rooted approaches into the public arena to confront racial and economic injustice. Efforts in states like Ohio, Florida, Missouri, Minnesota, New York and California are mobilizing several hundred faith leaders and congregations deeper into the arena of faith-rooted organizing. Troy Jackson and Nelson Pierce, playing an active role in the Ohio Prophetic Voices campaign, are building a statewide clergy network committed to moving a powerful prophetic narrative around racial and economic justice. Similarly, Isaiah in Minnesota is an independent network that has gone far beyond Alinsky in the area of goal-setting as well as in other aspects of its work.

Faith-rooted organizing offers a new horizon and a broader set of tools to unleash a poor-led movement for justice that is irrigated by the deepest wells of our faith traditions. When we extend ourselves beyond self-interest and treat people with dignity, we are able to dream together and act toward a new world. We are not concerned with merely winning short-term political victories but seek to change the culture of our cities, states, nation and world. We pursue a new social order, the social order Jesus describes in his teaching of the kingdom of God. Faith-rooted organizing gives us one action plan of how to get there, with the grace of God and the power of the Spirit.

The Moral Wisdom of Faith Traditions

As long as democracy is meted out by human hands and threaded through human hearts, we can't always assume that the best path will be chosen. That is why we need the moral wisdom that comes from faith traditions– and why it is important to organize from our deepest faith commitments.

Geographic distances and enormous diversity create an overwhelming challenge to a broad-based organizing approach. The Industrial Areas Foundation affiliates in Los Angeles, for example, have restructured multiple times but have never been able to replicate the impact they had in the Southwest. The disparate and economically unequal communities that make up Los Angeles County do not easily trust one another or identify common interests significant enough to compel sustained and dedicated action. Ethnic and racial conflict is endemic and often fierce. "Broad-based" organizing has been shown to not always be adequate for dealing with the kinds of racial conflict that surfaced in Alinsky's early Chicago experience.

In contrast to Alinsky-style organizing that seeks to amass power for power's sake, faith-rooted organizing asks "Power for what purpose?" What kind of community, society and world are we trying to create? Faith-rooted organizing is informed by a vision of the world founded in the Word of God. It imagines a new world based on the prophetic imagination of faith traditions and seeks to carve out a path of activism shaped by the values and virtues of these faith traditions.

In faith-rooted organizing, the community being organized is not completely free to determine its own values, boundaries or identity. Faith traditions and communities must continually examine their natural values in the light of the ideals of Scripture. The Bible offers visions, values and virtues that directly inform our organizing work.

In the Hebrew Scriptures and the New Testament, for example, there are nearly three thousand verses on poverty and justice.[7] When we are tempted to make decisions on the basis of narrow self-interest, the Scriptures call us to a collective worldview rooted in the love of neighbor and aflame with passion to build a beloved community.

Community organizing usually identifies common goals through the articulation of common problems that lend themselves to common solutions—the connection between private pain and public decisions. By contrast, the process of determining goals in faith-rooted organizing include deep and prayerful meditation on the Word of God. The Word gives us more than a list of values; it also eloquently describes the visions and dreams that God has for his people and his creation. The redemptive vision of Scripture provides a theological and moral orientation for our organizing work.

One way of articulating God's vision for our life together in community (and, more broadly, for the world) is *shalom*, a Hebrew term translated into English as "peace." Shalom means more than the cessation of conflict, however. Shalom assumes a prior commitment to justice among everything and everyone, from close friends to entire nations. To move beyond peace toward shalom means that our relationship to others and creation is fundamentally one of justice. We work for the time when "love and faithfulness meet together; righteousness and peace kiss each other" (Psalm 85:10).[8]

The Struggle for Shalom Justice

Faith-rooted organizing gathers people to work together for a just and sustainable world. Since justice has many different meanings, we must carefully analyze the concept.

The Hebrew term *mishpat*, best translated as "justice," is a multivalent term, embracing both juridical justice and fair social relations within a community. Lamentably, the King James Version often translates this as "judgment," blunting its radical social dimension.[9] But because the Torah frames its mystical revelation of God through a series of prophetic covenants that God establishes, the moral ideals explained in the Torah marry justice to peace and love, giving birth to shalom. And when Israel chose not to practice the justice of God (*mishpat*), the wrongdoing was seen as not only against the wronged individual, nor even only the community, but also a breaking of covenant with God. Injustice, Torah tells us, is fundamentally a violation against God.

The social dimension of *mishpat* included many different types of social relations. While always grounded in the covenantal relationship between Yahweh and Israel, it also referred to the relationship among Israelites within their tribe, their relationship with other nations and their relationship with the good creation. When nations dealt unjustly with Israel, Israel would cry out through passionate prayers for God's justice to be manifest. It was God and God alone who was the final arbiter of justice among the nations.

Similarly, when its marginalized people were neglected, Israel was guilty of injustice and subject to God's judgment. Prone to wander, Israel was constantly reminded of their obligation to care for those in need through prophets who preached the justice of God (e.g., Amos 5:21-24; Micah 6:6-8; Isaiah 1:17). Throughout the Hebrew Bible, kings and judges were judged by how they treated the weakest and most vulnerable in society. The God of Abraham, Jacob and Isaac was clearly on the side of the poor.

It is one thing to understand the importance of justice; it is another thing to put it into practice in our personal and political lives. In the Hebrew Bible the word *mishpat* is frequently paired with *sadiqah,* "right-eousness." Together they are the Bible's most common word pairing (e.g., Jeremiah 22:3-5; Isaiah 28:17-18), reinforcing the social dimension of justice. *Sadiqah* calls the people of Israel to do what is right. We can think of *sadiqah* as *mishpat* put into practice. *Mishpat* acknowledges everyone's basic human rights; *sadiqah* intentionally works for the establishment of right relations within the community. The conception of justice in the Hebrew Bible is thus not just a matter of personal morality but refers to how all people in the community, especially the marginalized, are treated.

The test of Israel's faith is the quality of their treatment of others. Justice is morality in its material form, lived out within the life of the community. Walter Brueggemann argues that the Hebrew Bible is an instruction manual on living shalom, "living in harmony and security toward the joy and well-being of every other creature."[10] Shalom is embedded into the created order and meant to be lived out in the lives of human communities in the broader ecological context.

As the people of God, Israel has a special responsibility to be bearers of shalom. The prophets continually respond to the cries of the oppressed for justice; they repeatedly remind Israel to consider how it is treating fellow humans and the earth. It is in working toward the materialization of justice and righteousness in the concrete details of life together, that Israel fulfills its destiny as a bearer of God's shalom.

Brueggemann describes shalom as "an enduring Sabbath of joy and well-being."[11] While practicing sabbath does entail resting, as God rested on the seventh day, the sabbath is fundamentally about God's justice— rest is possible because of the real presence of God's justice under the conditions of history. When sabbath is kept, oppression and exploitation can be ended, and there will be universal well-being throughout the whole community of creation. The sabbath is where God's shalom and justice converge.

Thus "shalom justice" describes the ultimate destination of creation.[12] The Year of Jubilee is a call to shalom justice, proclaiming liberty to slaves and the restoration of land (Leviticus 25). According to the Torah, there were four rules of the Jubilee year: (1) the land is to lie fallow; (2) debts are to be canceled; (3) slaves are to be freed; and (4) the land is to be re-turned or redistributed to its original holder (Leviticus 25:23-24). Simi-larly, in every seventh (sabbath) year the vineyards and orchards were to be left untended—not only so that the ground might be rejuvenated but also so that the poor might be provided for (Exodus 21:24; 23:10-11). The Deuteronomic law extends gleaning laws further, beyond the seventh year to each harvest season to extend this ethic of caring for the poor (Deuter-onomy 24:19-22). Consciously aligning himself with this prophetic tra-dition, Jesus framed his ministry around the Jubilee year of Leviticus 25 (Luke 4:18-20).[13]

Shalom justice is rooted in a worshipful acknowledgement that God the Creator is present in all creation and is graciously working for the redemption and reconciliation of the world. Since shalom is shattered in the community of creation through human sin and injustice, the search for shalom means joining the struggle for justice with wisdom and long-term commitment. As long as the dissonant din of powers and princi-palities, sin and suffering rings in the community of creation, the ministry of shalom justice is unfinished.

Native American theologian Randy Woodley argues that there is deep interconnectedness among all of the creatures of creation. There is a way of living—Woodley calls it the "Harmony Way"—that encompasses both being and doing in life according to an interconnected set of values that construct a meaningful whole. Harmonious and reconciled relations with others result when they are approached with a deep, ethical respect.[14] "Women," he says, "are sacred, children are sacred, no one is homeless." Values such as generosity and hospitality nurture a vision of a society "that is everything that we are hoping for—equity, a deep happiness and well-being for everyone—families, animals, earth, wind, and water."[15]

Like Woodley, Joerg Rieger, a German-born theologian living in Texas, sees shalom as the restoration of relationships that occurs when economic inequality is overcome. When a union contract stops the exploitation of low-wage workers, for example, it creates the context for mutual respect between management and labor. For Rieger, the image of the body of Christ in 1 Corinthians 12 further develops the vision of shalom; in order for the whole community to be whole and healthy, its "weaker" members must be recognized and supported as political subjects.[16] For Woodley and Rieger, building community is essential to God's transforming action in the world. They challenge us to discern where breakdowns to community occur and work to heal them.

The process of discerning God's vision for our community, society and world is not limited to reflection on Scripture, of course. Theologian Karl Barth said that we discern the will of God with a Bible in one hand and a newspaper in the other. Community organizing integrates the "newspaper" through the identification of common problems and common interests; faith-rooted organizing tries to see further, recognizing that human beings have goals that go beyond the solution of their problems and the easing of their personal pain. God gives his people dreams and visions; it is in the intersection between our everyday experiences, our own dreams and visions, and the scriptural plethora of poetic images that we find the dreams that can unite us in a common effort to create comprehensive change. When we know that our dreams are also God's dreams, we have a new sense of possibility and power to act.

By focusing on our dreams and visions, rather than our common problems, we also evoke a different spirit. A focus on common problems can be cathartic as well as bonding, helping people who have experienced the violation of invisibility to see and respect the importance of their own suffering and hence their own well-being. But it has been demonstrated that constant emphasis on remembering pain and agitating anger in community organizing wears people down physically. Counterbalancing pain and anger with faith and hope, prophetic imagination, inspiration and spiritual refreshment rejuvenates us as individuals and communities. Organizing around common dreams and visions refocuses our unity—long-oppressed and hopeless people are freed to be more positive and empowering, strengthened in faith and sustained for the struggle.

Justice in the Process and Justice in the End

It is critically important in faith-rooted organizing to ensure that not only the end result but the process meets God's goals for God's people. If the ultimate vision is shalom, the process of developing that vision must itself be just.

There is always a tension in the field of community organizing between internal goals (related to the development of the organization and the leaders within the organization) and external goals (related to objective institutional change and power shifts in the broader society). Years ago the Liberty Hill Foundation underwent a process to create an evaluation model for social change. In the process, they realized that internal and external goals were often in conflict.

For example, if an organization needs to field a speaker at city council, do they pick a veteran leader who can articulate effectively or a young leader who needs the opportunity to grow? The pressure to secure immediate wins in an ongoing social crisis can push an organization to subtly neglect the development of individuals and relationships, particularly those who least fit the dominant culture's definition of "valuable" leaders.

The biblical notion that each person is equally and infinitely precious, made in the image of God, informs this question for faith-rooted organizing. Enabling individuals to reach their full potential and building communities of justice are important regardless of their immediate impact. The commitment to realizing God's dream includes a commitment to lift up those who have been marginalized and create venues for the voices of those who have gone unheard. Thus faith-rooted organizing is committed to full power-sharing as an interim as well as an ultimate goal.

This commitment by necessity includes children and young people. Respect for children is an explicit scriptural mandate in and of itself, but in the full inclusion of the young in the organizing process is also an implicit recognition that the visions and dreams in Scripture cannot be achieved in one generation. The complete fulfillment of God's dreams will take multiple generations.

Recognizing the long arc of the work does not have to discourage us. We can still rejoice in every step forward toward beloved community. We must see every immediate victory, however, in the light of our ultimate goal. Reformation and revolution are ongoing processes, not events. Knowing that our goals will take generations to fully achieve necessitates a kind of faith and patience that is unfamiliar in a society addicted to instant rewards. Working on a dream that will take centuries to achieve frees us from the tyranny of the abusive pressure for quick results and gifts us with a biblical perspective that sustains hope even in the face of apparent defeat.

In the Philippines, workers in the sugar plantations have been trying to build a union for many years. Their Sugar Workers Union logo, Jesus with his fist raised, is an apt symbol for workers who labor long hours for so little pay that their children show signs of malnutrition. In 1987 I (Alexia) was able to spend some weeks with the sugar workers. An innovative young worker had initiated an act of creative resistance; to provide food for their children, she organized the women to plant banana trees around their huts. The managers of the plantation (run by an American corporation) sent guards to tear up the banana plants.

As the woman wailed, I asked the woman who organized the effort how she could continue in the face of such discouragement. She replied that she knew they would win.

Anguished and furious, I asked her "When will you win?"

"Soon," said the organizer.

"Are you crazy?!? What do you mean, 'soon'?"

"In the time of my daughter's daughter," she replied. "Soon."

Our task of building beloved community is inspired by Jesus' teaching of the kingdom of God, at once both a present and future reality. While Jesus inaugurated a new social reality, a new humanity, and a new heaven and earth, it is still not fully present. Thus, all of our attempts to build beloved community are corrupted with a human lust for power and apathy toward change. We long for an intimate and just community that is always a bit outside of our reach. But we do have foretastes of the feast to come. As theologian Darby Ray says, "The long-term horizon is important; the sense of God ahead but also in and through. It is the now and not yet."[17]

God's dream thus calls us forward and unites us in a vision of shalom justice. Faith-rooted organizing begins with the discernment together of this divine dream as it is born and reborn in our daily life together. The Holy Scriptures inspire us to dream and to dream big. Dr. King's "I Have a Dream" speech, which integrated the visions of the prophet Isaiah with his own personal dreams, is a reminder even today that shalom is coming to pass.

Immediately after the attacks of September 11, 2001, the U.S. tourism industry stalled and thousands of hotel workers were laid off. As the industry began to recover, luxury hotels around the country took advantage of the opportunity to "accelerate production" by not bringing back as many workers as they had laid off. Housekeeper workloads were increased to the breaking point—the point when disks literally slip and rupture, and backs began to break. Hotel workers in Santa Monica, California, led by the Hotel Employees and Restaurant Employees Union, organized to try to lower workloads and bring back more of their coworkers. They were up against titans—multinational companies with little to no stake in local communities. At one point when the struggle looked particularly hopeless, faith leaders held a Thanksgiving prayer service. Rabbi Neil Comess-Daniels brought a menorah and told the story of Nacshon.

Nacshon is the everyman of Jewish tradition. When the Hebrew slaves fled Egypt and arrived at the Red Sea, Jewish tradition says that Moses could not part the waters until Nacshon was willing to walk into water so deep that it came up to his nose and mouth. In the story of Hanukkah,

Nacshon is the person who believed that the oil would last eight days, manifesting the miracle that gave God's people the strength to triumph over their adversaries.

Rabbi Comess-Daniels connected the stories of Nacshon—stories of God's people's realized dreams for liberation—with the dreams of the hotel workers. With tears streaming down their faces, workers gave the rabbi a standing ovation. This dreaming had inspired and renewed them for the struggle.

That's what dreams do: they ignite our prophetic imagination. They give us a language that can unite and inspire us across racial, ethnic and religious differences, even across differences in societal power. Dreams bring people together, and when we organize our efforts based on our dreams and visions for our communities, the game often changes, and a different kind of agreement becomes possible.

•   •   •

Dear Alina and Yehsong:

You will have to set goals in order to achieve them, in organizing as in every other part of life. Don't limit yourself to goals that are too small or too focused on solving immediate problems. Let the deepest values of faith inform your goals.

Make a space for the people whom you organize to dream together for their lives, their community and their world. Help them to root their dreams in the power and beauty of God's dreams (particularly the dream of shalom). And don't be afraid to speak the language of dreams and visions to the powerful. Engage them in dreaming with you; you may be wonderfully surprised by the transformation that occurs.

3

Our Starting Place, the Call of the Poor

All organizing requires an analysis of the social context. You have to be aware of the current obstacles to the realization of your dream and the resources available to help you.

While every organizer analyzes their context, faith-rooted organizing by definition approaches that analysis with a different perspective. We see the world differently through the eyes of faith.

Dolores Huerta, the long-time vice president of the United Farmworkers, tells a story about when they had lost contracts covering 100,000 workers to the Teamsters, one of the most powerful unions in the country. She told Cesar Chavez that she knew that they had lost the struggle and it was time to admit defeat.

Cesar responded, "Dolores, now is the time to look through the eyes of faith." They continued the struggle and ultimately regained the lost contracts.

The reason the United Farmworkers held out until they won the struggle is because Chavez advocated for the movement to have faith in "things unseen," to not let short-term despair undercut long-term hope. An analysis that takes God's presence seriously is, consequently, often more hopeful than a secular analysis.

Nowhere is hope tested more fully than in the social context of the poor. It is appropriate, then, that the call of the poor is where faith-rooted organizing begins.

Prioritizing the Perspective of the Poor

One of the first interns at CLUE LA (who we'll call "Kate") came to us through a program at her Christian college that prepared students for urban ministry by immersing them in a poor community; they would live with a family there and volunteer for a faith-based service agency, development organization or advocacy ministry. Kate's family members were leaders in the evangelical church of her youth and active in the Republican Party in her home state. Her host family consisted of a single mother and her children, including a daughter Kate's age.

One night, President George W. Bush was on TV, and the daughter in Kate's host family began to throw shoes at the screen. Kate was furious at this sign of disrespect and a big argument ensued. I (Alexia) found out about it at 10:00 p.m., when Kate called me, angry and tearful, and demanded to be picked up immediately.

I picked Kate up and we drove around in circles through the Los Angeles night, wrestling with this conflict between Kate's perspective and the perspective of her host family. She went back and forth before suddenly blurting out, "Oh! I see."

"What do you see?" I asked.

"The status quo has always been good to me and my family, so we protect and honor it. The status quo has not been so good to my host family. I understand now."

Then I asked Kate, "How do you think Jesus sees the situation?"

Silence—the beginning of a profound transformation.

That night was Kate's dark night of the soul; she was able to unmask the lie within her own upbringing and psyche. As a young upper-middle-class white woman, she had benefited from the status quo, along with her family. Now she realized that the same status quo oppressed others. This personal crisis forced Kate to deepen her analysis of the causes of injustice and oppression. She had the courage to wrestle, like Jacob at

Peniel or Martin Luther King Jr. at his kitchen table. She demonstrated a commitment to work with and for a new identity. It was a moment of existential dislocation that enabled her to relocate her life in a vocation for justice.

Kate finished her internship and went on to become one of the most creative and effective faith-rooted organizers in the country, going back to her home state to cofound a nationally celebrated program saving the lives of migrant workers. Through her internship Kate learned the importance of listening and learning from the perspective of poor people, offering a different—and often more accurate—diagnosis of our current social situation.

Marshall Ganz, Harvard professor and long-time faith-rooted organizer, compares poor people to the canary in the coal mine. Coal mines often produce both methane and carbon monoxide, both which pose a risk to life if allowed to build up in poorly ventilated mine shafts. Before the advent of modern instruments to measure gas levels, miners commonly took a canary with them into the mines. The bird's small lungs were more sensitive to the poison gas, so when the canary keeled over, the miners knew they needed to flee the mine and vent the gasses. For Ganz, those at the bottom rung of any society often function as canaries in a mineshaft—barometers measuring whether the system is safe.

The comparsion is apt. From the lack of adequate health care to the housing crisis, the impact of social problems on the poor is evident long before the rest of us have to deal with it.

Why, then, is the perspective of the poor so often and so easily ignored? The movie *Bread and Roses* documents the struggle of Los Angeles janitors for living wages. In one scene two janitors are crouched down, working on a small area between an elevator and a hallway. The movie shows several sets of legs and briefcases proceeding down the hall, distant voices speaking, as they step right over the janitors without missing a beat. One janitor turns to the other and says "Did you know that we have magic powers?"

The other janitor is confused. "What magic powers could we possibly have?"

"The power to become invisible," he replied.

The invisibility of the poor is reinforced when the poor internalize their invisibility. This can have powerful negative consequences. As the Rev. Jesse Jackson once said, "If you believe that you can't do it, you can't do it." I'm reminded of another Jesse, a homeless peer chaplain in a program I directed in the late 1980s. Jesse had been a decorated Navy Seal in the Vietnam War. Involvement in drugs and alcohol led Jesse to a series of prison terms and then to the street. At the first activity of the homeless peer chaplain training program, a spiritual retreat at a retreat center in Lake Tahoe, Jesse was thumbing through the Good News version of the New Testament while he waited for the program to start. Suddenly he called the other trainees over to see what he had read.

"Look!" he said. "You gotta see this. Jesus came not to call the respectable people but the outcasts. He came to call us—us!"

In that moment Jesse saw his own potential for the first time in years. He saw himself as God sees him, not as a caged canary waiting to perish but as someone particularly worthy of a divine calling, particularly selected for great and good works.

The View from Below

Jesse's ultimate vision of himself as both broken and blessed is a truth that we all need to see about ourselves in order to be accurately humble and hopeful. In my first ministry, on a college campus, we loved to use an encounter between Jesus and a leper (Mark 1:40-45) as part of our evangelical outreach to students. When Jesus touched the leper, the students would invariably shudder; they were appropriately impressed by Jesus' courage. But when I used the same verse years later in a homeless drop-in center Bible study, participants didn't shudder; instead they heaved a deep sigh of relief. They didn't identify with Jesus; they identified with the leper. Their brokenness was confronted with Jesus' desire to bless them. For them as for all of us, facing the truth of our common human "leprosy" is a necessary first step in any process of healing and transformation.

The liberating trends in the great religious traditions often invert and subvert standard societal perspectives and corresponding beliefs. While most societies ascribe status to specific groups, allowing higher-status groups the right to define social reality and normative behavior, a consistent religious message is that the most accurate vantage point for viewing the world is from below. Religious texts are replete with reminders to not overlook the downtrodden, the maltreated, the powerless and the oppressed. There are ninety-two texts in the Old and New Testaments, for example, that speak of welcoming the stranger; many of them are directly related to the over six hundred scriptural passages on social and economic justice. Such repeated exhortations tell us that the common good is tied up in the needs and concerns of those at the bottom of society's ladder.

It's instructive to lift up a few of the most eloquent examples: In Luke 6:20, we read that the kingdom of God belongs to the poor. In 1 Corinthians 12:21-26, the author uses the metaphor of the special attention paid to parts of the body that are less socially approved to exhort readers to pay special attention and respect to the poor. The reason given is not that the poor are somehow wiser, more virtuous or more capable than others; rather this is the only way to avoid division in the body. Paul knows that the poor are likely to be forgotten and disrespected, so the only way to ensure that each person's gifts are fully utilized is to prioritize the perspective and gifts of the poor.

Rev. Timothy Dearborn, former senior staff of World Vision, notes that the only aspect of Jewish law that Paul mandates for the Galatians to observe is the injunction to remember the poor. Dearborn suggests that the body politic is often dismembered, with the poor and oppressed cut off and thrown aside. The re-membering of the body is thus an intentional reconnection of the poor and oppressed to the rest. The full reconnection only occurs when the poor are given priority.

Perhaps it is Hebrews that says it best: "Do not neglect to show hospitality to strangers, because you may entertain angels without knowing it" (Hebrews 13:2 NRSV). The New Testament term for "angels" means more than celestial beings; it can be directly translated as "messengers of God." The poor stranger that comes to the door seeking a bed for the night may well be a messenger of God, bringing a word and a blessing.

When we take seriously the ways in which the Scripture lifts up and emphasizes the perspective of the poor, we begin to read the whole Bible differently. The *Gospel in Solentiname* is a transcript of Bible studies that Fr. Ernesto Cardenal conducted with Nicaraguan peasants living in miserable poverty under the feudal economic policies of the Somoza dictatorship. Reading these transcripts is often disturbing for middle-class Americans, but the comments of the Bible study group are clearly rooted in an honest encounter between the Word of God and the daily life experiences of the poor. Here, for example, is an excerpt from a Bible study: "woe to you who are rich, because you have received your consolation. Woe to you who are full now, because you will be hungry. Woe to you who are laughing now for you will mourn and weep" (Luke 6:24-26 NRSV).

> *Fr. Cardenal:* It's curious that the reason these rich people were going to be punished was just because they had already had their joy, not for being evil rich people.

> *Tomas:* Maybe they are evil. Maybe they are people who are treating the poor people bad. . . . And they, maybe, instead of giving, maybe they take away. That's what they've been doing for some time, and we're abandoned. It seems like it can be that way.

> *Alejandro:* It's logical that the Gospel should put in this counterpart, because if it only said Beatitudes for the poor you might think that maybe there's another kind of Beatitudes for the rich. . . . Luke makes it clear that it's not that way. For Christ, humanity is divided into two well-defined classes, and he's in favor of one and against the other.

> *Laureano:* That's very revolutionary. He says that all those who are well off are going to be screwed. This turns the tables completely.

> *Olivia:* I think that what Jesus is condemning in them is lack of feeling. Because you have to have a hard heart to be happy while others are suffering, to be full of food while others are hungry— maybe the very people that work for them.

Marcelino: It wouldn't be so serious if they enjoyed wealth that came down from heaven, but their wealth is produced by the labor of others. A man has a cotton field of two thousand acres, but he doesn't farm two thousand acres. Other people farm the two thousand acres for him.

William: The prophets when they prophesied the future announced the salvation of the oppressed and the ruin of the oppressors.

Felipe: It seems to me that here Jesus has put himself on the side of the poor. But the Gospels can also be the liberation of the rich because this change, whether they like it or not, will make them fulfill the Gospels, even though by force. But we Christians must not wait for God to do this. We have to work for it. And I believe we have an obligation to work for the liberation of the rich. Some people say, 'What's it to us. Leave the rich the way they are, because they've got all they want!' but I believe that Christianity should preach to them. Christ did. It's clear that he also had rich people before him, because he's talking to them.

Alejandro: It's not as though when the revolution comes that they will be hungry or miserable. Nobody will be miserable then. But when they lose their property they're going to feel as though they're miserable as has happened to many who have left Cuba. And they're going to feel hunger, but it's only the hunger of their ambition.[1]

Jesus from Below

This theological strategy of reading Scripture from below is not only practiced in Latin America. Obery Hendricks Jr., in his book *The Politics of Jesus,* draws from a growing group of biblical scholarship called "Empire-Critical Studies" that looks at the Gospels and Jesus' life in the context of the Roman Empire. Hendricks understands Jesus as a poor Jewish peasant whose message of the kingdom of God was an allusion to Jubilee justice (Leviticus 25) and a critique of Roman Empire.[2] According to Hendricks, the Gospel writers sought to illuminate the teachings of

Christ as a hero of the people he suffered with. As jazz music was born of the impoverished sorrow of a blues people in the American South, Jesus' song of shalom was born in a poor Jewish community in Galilee, on the outer margins of the Roman Empire (Mark 1:10). Galilean Jews were despised by Jerusalem Jews and considered culturally inferior because they were from rural areas, had country accents, lived in a multicultural area and did not adhere strictly to Jewish law.[3] So, as a Galilean Jew, Jesus grew up experiencing poverty and persecution. As a result of his family's poverty, Jesus grew up with a deep empathic identification with the plight of other poor people, and his prophetic imagination was captured by the prophet's call to Israel to care for widows, orphans, strangers and poor (Zechariah 7:9-10).

"The kingdom of God has come near to you," proclaimed Jesus of Nazareth as he embarked on his three-year public ministry (Luke 10:9). In the Greek, *basileia tou theou* refers to the righteous reign of God, on earth as it is in heaven, unveiled in the presence of Jesus Christ. This reign is God-centered, rooted in the Hebrew notion of *Malkuth shamayim,* which refers to the sovereignty of God. Throughout his ministry, Jesus improvises on *malkuth shamayim,* which literally means the "sole sovereignty of the heavens."[4] God's "sole sovereignty of the heavens" for Jesus implies God's "sole sovereignty on earth," and his proclamation of the kingdom unveils that what is coming to pass from heaven is overtaking what is passing away on earth (1 Corinthians 7:31).

In the life of Jesus of Nazareth a new socio-economic order is born, a promissory presence for a coming, fundamentally just and compassionate future. Hendricks contends that Jesus' vision of the kingdom of God

> includes an egalitarian socio-economic order that takes responsibility for the well-being of all. It refuses to be hindered from the task of serving the needs of the dispossessed and the vulnerable by official sanctions, traditional narratives of social control, or even by edicts from on high, if they stand in the way of the kingdom's goal of ensuring that the basic elements of a healthy and secure life are available to all.[5]

For Hendricks, Jesus' teaching of the kingdom illuminated that God sees the needs of the poor and marginalized as holy. The Gospels are filled with accounts that afford the lower classes a theological subjectivity. Narratives and parables are filled with accounts of the masses: workers, fishermen, peasants and women.[6]

It is possible to find passages in Scripture that praise the elite. But such selective reading by itself doesn't characterize reading Scripture "from above." Such a hermeneutic goes further, reinforcing the power of the elites and interpreting subversive texts in ways consistent with the status quo. The priestly order of Jesus' time, for example, interpreted the Law as advocating religious legalism, effectively elevating their socio-economic status. Old Testament prophetic critiques of the ruling classes of Israel—such as the biting critiques of Isaiah, Amos and Micah—are stripped of their poignancy when read from above and rendered benign. It is only when read from below that their radical intent is revealed (or not suppressed).

Citing psychiatrist Franz Fanon, Hendricks likens the oppression under Roman rule to reactionary psychosis, or post-traumatic stress in war-torn areas, where he observed an increased incidence of exorcisms. Hendricks picks up on Fanon's insight in his interpretation of the Gerasene demoniac. When Jesus arrived in the country of Gerasenes, he met a demon-possessed man who was homeless, living in the tombs on the outskirts of town (Luke 8:26-39). The man was wild and could not be bound by chains; he repeatedly injured himself, cutting himself up with rocks. The community was scared of this man, but Jesus had compassion on him. When Jesus asked him his name, he responded, "Legion," for many demons had entered him. Then Jesus cast the demon Legion out of the man, sending it into pigs who drowned in the sea.

During that time the name "Legion" would have immediately called to mind the legions of the Roman Army. By calling this demon by name, Jesus is not only saving a demon-possessed man, but he is critiquing the Roman political occupation and the oppression that has developed in its wake. During a colonial occupation, the colonized people often internalize self-hatred and begin to act out in self-destructive ways. In the context of first-century Israel, even the casual listener would identify the

Roman legions as the demons who disrupt the peace of their community.[7]

Jesus' claims to be the Son of God were particularly disruptive to Roman rule, as well as to the temple ideology of Jerusalem Jews. Writing in the first century, Jewish historian Josephus demonstrated how the priestly class benefitted from their reinforcement of Roman rule. He recounts how, when people protested the lavish lifestyle of the priestly order, the priests would often resort to violence. Yeshua ben Hananiah, for example, was scourged until his bones showed for protesting priestly corruption.[8] Similarly, Jesus' claims to be the "true vine" that makes the people pure by his word (John 15) function as a prophetic indictment of the temple priests. His emphasis on the kingdom and obeying the will of God would be understood as delegitimating both imperial and corrupt religious powers. And while the Pharisees were consumed with worldly riches, Jesus emphasized heavenly treasure (Matthew 23:23) and sided with the prophets in his compassionate commitment to the poor.[9]

In summary, reading the Bible from below, in the context of the socioeconomic issues and conditions of its time, gives us an understanding of how people would have understood Jesus' prophetic teaching. Even his exorcisms and healings function as symbolic critiques of the ruling powers of Jewish life. Within the scribal culture of the day, the notion of teaching—especially when coupled with the kind of authority that Jesus claimed—could rightly be construed as social and political power. Jesus' teaching, however, incited the deepest desires and dreams of liberation from oppression. Throughout his ministry Jesus incited the poor in northern Galilee, who were often discriminated against by the hierarchy of the Jerusalem Temple, to claim their own power. And by engaging in direct encounters with all pretenders to the throne, whether their power plays were political or religious, Jesus offered a prophetic critique of the powers of his day.

Practical and Emotional Implications

To prioritize the perspective of the poor for the sake of the common good implies that we cannot give the same weight to everyone's analysis of social problems and solutions. All voices are important, but not all voices speak the truth in a way that reveals that which we most need to know about social reality and the process of change. What the privileged often fail to see and recognize in everyday life is what is most important.

Standard community organizing methods rely on a series of "one-on-ones" (individual interviews) to determine the issues that the group should take on. Faith-rooted organizing recognizes that not all "one-on-ones" should be weighted equally. The first faith-rooted litmus test for an issue is how it impacts the poor—according to the perspective of the poor themselves.

Oppressed people see the world differently than their oppressors. Even good and just business owners see the world differently than their workers. Economic justice is an issue that is existentially important to the poor—and not often on the priority list for the privileged.

Maria, a single mother with two children, worked for a luxury hotel in downtown Los Angeles for eight years, cleaning sixteen hotel rooms a day. After eight years she earned an average monthly wage of $1,300, well under the poverty line. (Maria is not alone: roughly a third of the residents of Los Angeles County are working poor.) As rents climbed, her low wages led her to move an hour-long bus ride away to be able to afford an apartment. Unfortunately, the rent on the new apartment also continued to climb—from $650 per month when she moved in to $1,200 per month.

When her children began to complain of hunger, Maria began to look for a second job. However, she had a dilemma. Her deepest desire was to help her children do well in school and stay out of gangs so they would have a better life than she'd had; leaving them alone in the evening could threaten that dream. She had state-subsidized child care for her day job but would have to pay the going rate—about $600 per month per child— to cover the hours she would work a second job. She had to decide between ensuring that her children would have enough to eat and ensuring that they would have care and protection in the evening.

As Maria struggled with her decision, the CEO of her hotel chain reported annual wages of $20 million (plus stock options). He is not alone either: in 1970, the average U.S. CEO earned 30 times more than his lowest-paid workers; in 2005, he earned 411 times more.[10] Maria and her CEO see the world and make decisions in it according to very different priorities.

Maria and her CEO don't just differ at the level of their cognitive perspective; how they experience reality emotionally differs as well. Often the church wants to bring these two perspectives together in a neutral way, but is it really possible for a spindly child to sit down and negotiate in an emotionally neutral way with a bully, or for a rape victim to sit down and make peace with her rapist? Negotiations between a poor worker who can't pay rent and food, and a business owner who continues to take more than a reasonable percentage of the company's profits, hardly seem neutral. A more spiritually accurate emotional response to such a contrast is prophetic rage, and if that rage is suppressed, the violation is doubled. If the anger is acknowledged as legitimate, however, it often transmutes into determination.

Lupe, a hotel housekeeper whose spine is severely damaged from "the acceleration of production" in her hotel, lived in numb submission for years. Unable to sit, stand or lie down without pain, she could not carry her children or grandchildren. When she began to awaken to the injustice of her situation, her first response was prophetic rage. Over time, partially because of her Christian faith, she drew sustaining energy from her firm resolve that no other woman would have to suffer what she has suffered.

Lupe's passionate determination is one of the core gifts of the perspective of the poor. The prophetic anger of (and for) the poor, and its expression in a struggle for justice, is often the force that first makes the poor visible. Clara, a housekeeper at the Doubletree Hotel in Santa Monica, California, had done the same backbreaking work day in and day out for seven years, never receiving a raise because she had never received an evaluation. One day, Clara became involved with a union organizing campaign at the hotel. Her involvement changed her life before they had won even a single objective victory. "For the seven years that I worked at the Doubletree," she told me, "no one in management ever greeted me in the hall; no one ever acknowledged my existence. After I got involved with the campaign, they greeted me by name! They invited me into their offices for a discussion. It was uncomfortable to be challenged but it was wonderful to be seen."

Rev. Phil Lawson, a civil rights leader and Methodist pastor, recalls that in the early days of Lyndon Johnson's War Against Poverty and the formation of the Black Panther Party, Jeremiah 1:10 became very meaningful to him. In that verse, Jeremiah laments that he is only a youth; God responds by touching his mouth and telling him that he is called and empowered "over nations and over kingdoms, to pluck up and to pull down, to destroy and to overthrow, to build and to plant." Rev. Lawson saw in that verse that the youth of the day were being called to uproot in order that there might be a new and healthier planting. He recalls one instance in which a formal discussion about the distribution of public funds was expanded to involve the "maximum participation of the poor."

> All these city council committees that were making decisions about this money, how it was going to be spent, had to have poor people on them. And the moment the poor people got there, they busted open the whole discussion. There was no decorum. There was no Robert's Rules of Order. One of the greatest benefits of the war on poverty was that city halls and city structures across America got broken open by poor whites and poor Blacks who had to come in and made sure their voices were going to be heard. . . . In Kansas City council meetings would go until 2, 3, 4 o'clock in the morning because poor people were getting involved . . . up and down the line.[11]

Those who sit on top of the power structure are not comfortable with uprooting. As Rev. Lawson suggests, the best response to such discomfort is to follow Jesus.

> Jesus was wide open. He allowed anyone to be a part of his fellowship, his table, regardless of what other people said about them. He developed a relationship on his own. Don't take other people's word for it when they say you should not know these people. You should stay away from these people. You shouldn't go to these places. All these should-nots are not keeping with love and God who wants you to become, to evolve, to grow. Hook into Jesus above everything else. And you'll notice that Jesus became partnered with the least, the lost and the last. The people at the bottom of society, Jesus spent most of his time with them. He was in solidarity with them.[12]

The Dance of Solidarity

If the city council of Kansas City in the 1960s, or the CEOS of the corporations where Lupe, Clara and Maria worked, were asked about the most significant problems facing our society, they would answer very differently than if you were to ask the poor. Modern society tends to value the perspective of employers and authority figures more than that of low-wage workers; their success is seen as evidence of their wisdom and worth. We often ask about a person's wealth using the phrase, "What is he worth?" The Scriptures tell us, however, that believing that some people are worth more than others is not true or right. We stand on an ancient tradition, resonant around the globe and throughout the ages, that states that every human being is equally and infinitely valuable.

While recognizing the value of every vantage point, faith-rooted organizing also understands that a fair hearing of differing perspectives is necessary for truth to emerge. Fair hearings for those with low social status are hard to come by, however. In contrast to a society that gives inordinate weight to the perspective of those with more social status, we read in 1 Corinthians 1 that "God chose what is foolish in the world to shame the wise; God chose what is weak in the world to shame the strong; God chose what is low and despised in the world, things that are not, to reduce to nothing things that are, so that no one might boast in the presence of God" (1 Corinthians 1:27-29 NRSV). To prioritize the perspective of the poor for the sake of the common good does not imply the devaluing of the gifts of those who are not poor. Instead, it acknowledges the necessity of the dance of solidarity.

Solidarity is a term commonly used in Latin America to describe the commitment and engagement of those who are not poor in struggles for justice. Joerg Rieger speaks of deep solidarity as rooted in the recognition that "we are really in the same boat. The system that is not benefitting the poor is not benefitting us either. Jesus goes out to the lost sheep, the lost son and yells at the holders of privilege."[13] Those who are engaged in solidarity are committed to a partnership with the poor that rectifies the imbalances of our society. Solidarity does not imply a superior virtue. It is, rather, a matter of recognizing the need for the gifts and leadership of the poor in the struggle to create the beloved community that will bless us all.

Solidarity recognizes that in order to attain a just world there must be a radical shift of power relationships even within the movement for justice; if there is not justice in the process, there will not be justice in the end. In 2012, I (Alexia) was training a group of InterVarsity staff in Mexico City for the Urban Projects and Global Projects networks. They already understood solidarity on a certain level—they believed in the importance of immersing themselves in poor communities and in attending to the needs of their poor neighbors. My task was to help them to fully understand their *partnership* with the poor.

We began by asking them to write down on an index card an experience where they had ministered to someone who is poor. We arranged the index cards in a heart shape on a white board. We then asked them to identify a poor person who had ministered to them, directly or indirectly. They wrote the names of these people on tea candles, lighting each candle as they related the stories of these encounters and relationships. These exercises formed the basis for a deeper conversation about the tendency to see poor people primarily as victims needing assistance, rather than recognizing their full spiritual giftedness and calling. We then took some time to reflect on positive experiences of partnership between poorer and more privileged believers and to analyze the necessary ingredients for developing powerful partnerships. We also identified some of the cultural and institutional threats that get in the way—the undercurrents that cause some people to gravitate toward center stage and others to hold back from full participation or leadership. By the end of the session, staff who had been raised in poverty were able to share their feelings and experiences openly with their colleagues in new ways. The dance of solidarity had been taught; the dance music had started to play.

Saul Alinsky and his disciples have often sneered at solidarity, seeing it as a weaker motivation than self-interest. But during the civil rights movement, solidarity was a strong motivation: young people from the North were beaten, imprisoned and even murdered in the cause of justice for African Americans in the South. In the Central American Sanctuary Movement, solidarity caused faith leaders to repeatedly risk arrest and prosecution to stand with foreigners who would potentially face death squads if deported. Solidarity requires love that is so passionate that it will not stop giving until the dreams of the beloved one are real. As Che Guevara said, "The true revolutionary is motivated by great feelings of love."[14]

Solidarity is not simple or easy, either for the poor or for the nonpoor; it is best done in a spirit of love and grace—with plenty of room for tears and laughter. Integrating the full gifts of everyone while prioritizing the perspective of the poor is more art than science. If shalom is built upon righteousness and mercy, solidarity is built through vulnerability and trust. Because of the stress involved in resisting power structures, we have to be able to articulate its impact on us. And when our fellow organizers come to us with stories of anxiety, fear and fatigue, we must listen generously.

When we trust enough to be vulnerable with one another, walls come down quickly. In the late 1980s, an intentional community of common mission was formed among the homeless peer chaplain volunteers and non-homeless congregational volunteers in the Berkeley Ecumenical Chaplaincy to the Homeless. One technique for building the community was to pair homeless leaders and non-homeless volunteers, asking them to answer a personal question about their childhoods. "Fran," an elderly, patrician woman from generations of wealth, was paired with "Ernie," a homeless ex-con from a "trailer-trash" family in the South. It turned out that they had both spent their childhoods terrified of an alcoholic uncle. In the outside world, Fran would never have seen a homeless man like Ernie as a leader worthy of respect. However, the bond created through their relationship laid the foundation for Fran to respect Ernie's leadership, and for Ernie to call upon Fran's gifts without surrendering his leadership role in that ministry.

In 2010, in Costa Mesa, California (a city famous for its anti-immigrant policies), CLUE Orange County brought immigrant evangelical pastors and mainstream megachurch pastors together for a prayer breakfast and dialogue on immigration. The immigrant pastors shared the struggles of their congregations, with many families facing the threat of separation through deportation. The mainstream pastors likewise shared their struggle to address immigration issues without losing members. A powerful bond began to form between them when Juan Martinez, dean of

Hispanic ministry studies at Fuller Theological Seminary, called the group to realize that they were all afraid, and that they shared the conviction that the cross of Christ calls us to overcome our fears.

A commitment to solidarity often requires the development of structures which intentionally equalize power. According to religion professor Sharon Welch, recent research shows that the balance of power shifts only when at least 15 percent of the leadership represents a disadvantaged group. As Justo Gonzalez lays out powerfully in his Bible study on Acts 6, there was a power difference in the early church between the Hebrews and the Hellenists. Those who had come from Jewish communities in Greek cities (the Hellenists) complained that the widows from Israel (Hebrews) were getting more of the daily distribution of food than they were. And all of the apostles—the council of leaders—were Hebrews! The apostles appointed seven Hellenist leaders to ensure that the daily distribution was equal. The council's decision was amazing—how many leadership groups so voluntarily give so much power over to underdogs?

The practice of equalizing power is not confined to the ancient world. In the early 1990s, there were three distinct groups making up the Oakland Catholic Worker community: U.S. citizens (many of whom were faith leaders), educated Central American refugees from urban areas (most of whom had fled as student leaders), and *campesinos* from the countryside (many of whom had fled massacres.) The leadership gradually realized that the *campesinos* almost never spoke in community meetings. So they created a structure in which the *campesinas* (women from the countryside) met first for an hour and were then joined by the *campesinos*. After another hour passed, they were joined by the educated refugees. Finally the U.S. citizens joined in for the formal meeting. The full group sat in an oval, with bilingual members at the ends and monolingual members close to the center. Two translators sat at the center, ensuring that everyone could speak freely. The meetings came alive, with everyone throwing in concerns, ideas and suggestions. Solidarity became a reality, and the perspective of the poor was prioritized in a way that helped to attain the common good.

In faith-rooted organizing it is important that organizing work be led by people who are most affected by the present injustice. The Kensington Welfare Rights Union (KWRU), for example, was founded in April 1991 when six women on welfare in Philadelphia's Kensington neighborhood (the poorest in Pennsylvania) came together to try and figure out how to meet their needs together. The six women—Alexis Baptist, Sandy Brennan, Diane Coyett, Cheri Honkala, Louis Mayberry and Debra Witzman—took over the office of the Department of Public Welfare, were arrested and were taken to prison. The news media called it a "witch hunt"; the women were tried and found not guilty. In the process they were able to lift up their neighborhood's struggle and give it nationwide publicity.[15]

The organization grew as they fought in the courts and in city, state and national politics for their rights, for survival and for dignity in the welfare bureaucracy. They succeeded in part because they were led by the affected group—single mothers on welfare.

Seeing common cause in their concerns (many welfare mothers eventually become homeless) the KWRU built on earlier work by the National Union of the Homeless, an organization by and for the homeless. Tactics like tent cities had been used effectively by faith-rooted organizers as far back as Resurrection City in 1968, when thousands of poor people camped out on the national mall in Washington, D.C. Out of the Kensington tent city protest in Philadelphia in 1995, a much bigger protest would emerge the following year, when eighty homeless families took over an abandoned Catholic Church in north Philadelphia.

St. Edward's church, formerly an important center of the community, had been vacant for years after a wave of closures of low-income parishes across the city. The takeover was met with a strong negative reaction from the city and Catholic diocese but an even stronger surge of support from neighbors, poor and homeless families, and allies from across the city. As union supporters celebrated communion together in the shell of this church, many people experienced a profound conversion—a *kairos* moment suggesting new possibilities for their lives.[16] Many KWRU families eventually secured housing as a result of the campaign.

The leadership developed through this struggle has continued to bear fruit for many years. "The takeover of St. Ed's Church," says Liz Theo-

haris, a leader from the KWRU, "is the birthplace of a poor-led movement
to end poverty foregrounding the church's ministry of love and justice."[17]
In 1999 the KWRU helped to found the Poor People's Economic Human
Rights Campaign, which evolved into a network of over a hundred grassroots organizations, community groups and nonprofit organizations. In
May 2003 Liz Theoharis and Willie Baptist[18] established the Poverty Initiative at Union Theological Seminary in New York City with Chris
Caruso, Amy Gopp, Dawn Plummer and Alix Webb. In 2006, the Poverty
Initiative launched and then expanded the Poverty Scholars Program,
with a focus on bringing together grassroots leaders from around the
country to share experiences, develop strategy, deepen knowledge about
the problems they're facing and break their isolation by building ties with
other organizers and organizations.

Working with Joe Strife and other faith-rooted organizers in the student
group Empty the Shelters, Theoharis recruited students from the University of Pennsylvania, Villanova University, the Community College of
Philadelphia and others. For many years the student organizing that resulted was based at a house called Jubilee, which was part of the Life
Center Association, a network of intentional community/cohousing
created by the Movement for a New Society (MNS). MNS was a social
justice movement led by (among others) Dale T. Irvin, president of New
York Theological Seminary (who completed his doctorate at Union Theological Seminary). With this wide network and long tradition of faith-
rooted organizing behind them, and with the help of social justice ministers like William Sloan Coffin, Baptist and Theoharis were able to
institutionalize the work of ending poverty at Union Theological Seminary under the administration of President Joseph Hough.

A group of students from Eastern University were also transformed by
their experience in St. Edward's church. They went on to form the Simple
Way, which has become a national leader in raising issues of poverty and
justice in the evangelical community and beyond. During the takeover of
St. Ed's, Shane Claiborne and other leaders at Eastern contacted their
friends and invited them to go down and do something about it. When
the carload of college students got to the church they met the homeless

families and decided to the join the struggle. They returned to Eastern, plastering the campus with fliers and making announcements from their cafeteria tables: "Jesus is being evicted from a church in North Philly!" Nearly eighty Eastern students joined the protest.

Since that day St. Ed's has been a spiritual home for the Simple Way. Shane and his wife Katie Jo were married there, as were two other Simple Way founders, Michael and Michelle Brix. Shane Claiborne writes,

> It was in St. Ed's that I was born again . . . again. There is something mystical about finding God in the ruins of the church. At the same time, I had no idea who St. Francis of Assisi was, but somehow the divine whisper that he and those young radicals heard in Italy in the thirteenth century was very familiar: "Repair my church which is in ruins." Now hundreds of years later, another bunch of young dreamers was leaving the Christianity that smothered them, to find God in the abandoned places, in the desert of the inner city. I felt so thirsty for God, so embarrassed by Christianity, and so ready for something more.[19]

Six of the Eastern students who went to St. Ed's eventually moved into a Kensington row house with a vision of living life together after the model of church in Acts 2. These new urban monastics, and others like them throughout the United States, go deep into the spiritual and liturgical traditions of the church to find spiritual resources to sustain the struggle. In 2005 they drafted a list of "Twelve Marks" of Christian practice in the contemporary world; more recently they put together *Common Prayer,* a resource putting the global struggle for justice hand-in-hand with ancient liturgies.[20] Folks at the Simple Way talk about the importance of exegeting not only Scripture but your neighborhood. They are actively involved in local organizing efforts around gun violence, anti-homeless legislation, urban greening and have a strong national and international presence around Gospel-living, peacemaking and anti-militarism.

United Church of Christ minister Noelle Damico is another faith-rooted organizer whose prophetic ministry is rooted in the priority of the perspective of the poor. She has been one of the lead organizers of faith leaders to join with the Coalition of Immokalee Workers, a community-based organization of mainly Latino, Mayan Indian and Haitian immigrants working in low-wage jobs throughout the state of Florida.[21] Immokalee, Florida, is one of the poorest towns in the United States. The corporate food industry purchases a high volume of fruits and vegetables, leveraging its buying power to demand cheap prices from its suppliers, which often leads to low wages and poor working conditions for the farmers. Many have described the oppressive treatment of the farmers there as modern-day slavery.

Amid such unjust working conditions, the Coalition has moblilized with ferocity, providing one of the best examples of a poor-led movement for justice. The coalition launched a national boycott of Taco Bell, calling on the fast-food giant to take responsibility for human rights abuses in the fields where its produce is grown and picked. Damico organized faith leaders in Protestant denominations like the Presbyterian Church (USA), the United Church of Christ and the Christian Church (Disciples of Christ). I (Peter) joined in after hearing the resolution pass in the General Assembly for my demonination, the Christian Church (Disciples of Christ). Even though I had lived on 7-Layer Burritos during my years at Wheaton College, I refused to darken the door of Taco Bell for four years, and in that small act of self-denial I felt a sense of solidarity with the farmers in Florida.

Since the owners of Taco Bell were Roman Catholic, they were moved by the mobilization of the faith community. In protests and marches, faith leaders would lift up Scriptures like this exhortation from the Epistle of James: "Look! The wages you failed to pay the workers who mowed your fields are crying out against you. The cries of the harvesters have reached the ears of the Lord Almighty" (James 5:4). The farmers cried out to the corporate executives, but when faith leaders joined the struggle it made a big difference—showing just how vital it is for faith leaders to follow the leadership of the poor, joining their struggle for justice with fervent prayer and courageous support.

The Taco Bell boycott gained broad student, religious, labor and community support over the course of four years. In March 2005, amidst growing pressure, Taco Bell agreed to meet all of the demands of the

Coalition of Immokalee Workers to improve wages and working conditions for Florida tomato pickers in its supply chain. And after the successful conclusion of the Taco Bell boycott, the Coalition of Immokalee Workers has been able to convince companies such as Subway, McDonald's and Whole Foods to pay fair wages. As Shane Claiborne said, "The Coalition of Immokalee Workers is one of the most gracious and successful poor-led, faith-rooted movements for economic justice. They bring together seamlessly the streams of King and the Civil Rights Movement and Chavez and the Farmers Movement."[22]

Faith-rooted organizing is a continuation of the unfinished business of King's poor people's campaign. It gathers a growing group of ordinary radicals from all social classes and positions for the work of social transformation. The power of the kingdom of God in history is the power of the crucified Savior, incarnate in the least of these (Matthew 25:31-46). Faith-rooted organizers walk alongside the poor, working together for a more just and sustainable future. From the poor who discover their agency, to the wealthy who discover solidarity in the cause of the oppressed, to the oppressors who hear God's demands for justice, faith-rooted organizing is fertile ground for conversion. These conversions happen every day—as demonstrated in our own lives.

I (Peter) was born again during the summer of 1985, at Christian Youth Fellowship summer camp in Morton, Mississippi. We gathered down by the lake under a star-filled sky, and someone played the guitar as we sang hymns and praise songs together. I cried out to God and was filled with the Holy Spirit from head to toe. The next Sunday my Pastor Robin Ballard had an altar call at First Christian Church in Vicksburg, Mississippi. I charged forward and accepted Jesus as my Savior and Lord. From that day on, I have done my best to follow in the footsteps of Jesus. But I was "born again . . . again" as a thirty-one year old man in New York City, shortly after September 11, 2001. It was in the dust of death at Ground Zero in Lower Manhattan. I was volunteering as a chaplain serving rescue workers, fire fighters and police officers. Breathing in the eviscerated flesh of my fellow humans, I had a baptism by fire that both broke my heart and emboldened me to work for peace and justice in the world. Ever since that experience, I have sought to be a prophetic minister for justice, including ministering with Seamen's Church Institute of New York and New Jersey, organizing clergy to keep Walmart out of New Jersey, cofounding the Micah Institute at New York Theological Seminary, organizing clergy in the Living Wage NYC Campaign, and pastoring at Park Avenue Christian Church. My justice conversion in New York City in 2001 changed the direction of my life forever.

Faith-rooted organizing requires that we prioritize the perspective of the poor for the sake of the common good. It calls for processes and structures in our organizing that ensure that this perspective is consistent in word and deed. When we discern our issues, we must begin with the question, "Whose voices are present in this conversation, and who is being excluded? How can we respect and support the leadership of those most affected by this issue? How can the poor lead the process of organizing from analysis to advocacy?" Faith-rooted organizing is a poor-led movement for justice, involving conversion on all sides.

• • •

Dear Alina and Yehsong:

If you want your analysis to be divinely accurate, see through the eyes of the poor. If you do this correctly, you will not hate or even dismiss the privileged but rather see clearly how to create the dance of solidarity.

4

Discerning the *Kairos*

A vision is not a plan. This sounds simple, but anyone who has done any organizing work knows that the translation of mystical vision into an effective prophetic plan is hard work. In order to create change, we have to move from the identification of our common dream to a strategic focus on immediate issues with clear objectives.

The faith-rooted understanding of how to discern which issue to address is significantly different from the process used by Alinsky-based community organizing models. These decide on an issue by asking members of organizations to articulate, pare down and then choose a common self-interest. In faith-rooted organizing, issues are not decided; they are discerned. The process of discernment helps us to push through the dark clouds of fear and fatigue that skew our agenda. Instead we are caught up in the bright clarity of God's *kairos*.

Kairos is one of two Greek words used to describe time. The other word, *chronos*, refers to the sequence of hours and minutes, days and years (*chronological* time). In the New Testament, *kairos* refers to a different sort of time, a moment in history when God intervenes and change dramatically occurs. On multiple occasions, from the wedding at Cana to the outskirts of Jerusalem, Jesus says that he cannot do what others want him to do because his *kairos* has not yet come. The apostle Paul writes to the

Roman church that "at just the right *kairos,* when we were still powerless, Jesus died for the ungodly" (Romans 5:6).

The moment Rosa Parks refused to move to the back of the bus, in defiance of a racist law in Montgomery, Alabama, was a *kairos* moment. In this small, simple act all of the forces working for change culminated, and the civil rights movement leapt forward. This is not to say that God ordained segregation but rather that the multiple injustices occurring at that moment in history could be best addressed through the revelatory issue of segregation. A *kairos* issue reveals the deeply held lies that justify a pattern of injustice and opens up the space for God's truth to combat those lies directly. *Kairos* issues have the capacity to move whole lives and communities forward toward a more just society.

Kairos issues are pivotal, catalyzing the solution of a multitude of problems. The *kairos* issue is what the whole community discerns as key to moving a social movement forward, allowing shalom justice to take root in a specific time and place.

The Lie, the Divine Truth and the Issue That Reveals

Selecting the segregation of buses and lunch counters as key issues for the civil rights movement was linked to a process that James M. Lawson brought back from the Ghandian movement in India. The discernment process begins with the identification of a lie that is believed by the majority of the people in a given society at a given historical moment. This lie is commonly used to justify systemic injustice and evil. In the civil rights movement, a number of leaders determined that this big lie was the belief that some people were worth more than others. Among other things, this lie had been used to justify slavery, in the assumption that some people were born to serve and others to be served.

Charlie Sherrod, civil rights leader from Alabama, speaks poignantly about the process through which he came to realize that he was not intrinsically inferior to white people.

> Now I believed when I was a boy, 14 years old, that white people
> knew everything. White folk, they made no mistakes; they were in

charge of everything. That put me in second class citizenship. But then I went to this meeting, interracial meeting, and I'm listening and I think, "what, she don't know that?" These are white people. White people know everything. Why don't they know that? So then I started reading, and I read and I read and I read. . . . They have lied to me all my life. . . . So I went into the movement, thinking and believing a little bit more and a little bit more in myself. . . . All my life always believing in God but not really believing in myself, in God in me.[1]

After discerning the lie, it is necessary to then identify the clearest manifestation of the lie. Civil rights leaders saw segregation as the clearest contemporary manifestation of the lie. That made segregation the movement's *kairos* issue: confronting segregation would unlock and empower the fight for justice in all areas of life.

When Lawson eventually cofounded Clergy and Laity United for Economic Justice (CLUE) in 1996, he believed that one of the clearest manifestations of the lie in the 1990s was the crisis of working poverty. The belief that some workers' children were worthy of health insurance, while other workers' children were not, was clearly based on the same assumption about relative human value. Later still Lawson appealed to the same lie when he called CLUE to engage in the struggle for immigration reform. Different *kairos* issues, same lie.

One of the special roles that people of faith have in the struggle for justice is the eloquent articulation of eternal truths that confront these deep-seated lies. The values that emerge from these eternal truths are not optional but rather rooted in the nature of reality and the fabric of the universe. When a presenting issue is won without the overarching lie being discredited, the same injustice will grow back in a different form. Many victories, but the same stubborn lie survives.

Common Lies

In recent years, faith-rooted organizing groups around the United States have been asking themselves about the lies that justify injustice and the

biblical truths that counteract them. While each community is different
and uses different language and expressions to articulate the lie, there are
common threads.

Many communities have identified the lie that "those who have more
materials goods deserve their wealth and those who are poor, their
poverty." While there is scriptural support for the idea that prosperity is
a blessing from God, there are plenty of passages that portray poverty as
either the result of injustices committed by those who are not poor, or a
spiritual opportunity to become an agent of change.

Others have discerned that the key lie in their community is that "we
are not connected and not responsible for one another's well-being."
Rabbi Leonard Beerman, a lifelong faith-rooted activist who assisted the
peace talks in Paris that ended the Vietnam War, expresses the implications of our common connection:

> Whatever I can do or say to make my partner feel better about
> herself works to my selfish advantage and whatever I do or say to
> make her feel worse about herself works to my personal disad-
> vantage. And I think that applies to individual couples but it also
> applies to people in general and to nations . . . make them feel
> more worthy, more valued, more honorable, more beautiful,
> whatever. Whatever I do to diminish those we call our enemies
> works against us.[2]

Still other communities have focused on "the threat of the other," in
which the stranger is seen as a source of danger instead of a portal of
blessing. This lie is at the root of much anti-immigrant sentiment, but it
is powerfully subverted by the story in Genesis 18 about angels who come
to Abraham and Sarah as strangers, as well as in Hebrews 13:1-2, which
states that any stranger may be an angel in disguise.

Pervasive throughout the Global North (and particularly strong in the
United States) is the old adage that "each person can and should lift
himself or herself up by the bootstraps; we don't need anyone else." While
this rugged individualism has had a positive impact at many moments
throughout history, without correction by Christian values it echoes the

most fundamental lie of all: our lives belong to us and not to the Lord of heaven and earth who created and sustains us.

Some communities express a commitment to care for the vulnerable and protect human rights but ignore a persistent injustice occurring in their midst. For example, they may disregard the anguish of the working poor because they are too busy taking on issues such as marriage equality, green business practices or international peace. Their logic is often rooted in the lie that "there is not enough room in the boat for everyone"—an alternative form of the lie of scarcity. This fear-based impulse is counteracted by the promise of abundance threaded throughout the Old and New Testament and powerfully articulated in John 10:10: "I have come that you may have life in abundance."

Often groups have pressing issues that they are already working on; they do not feel the need to discern new issues. But identifying and articulating the lies and universal truths embodied in their issue is still important: it roots their issue in sacred ground held in common by others outside their group. Often when public leaders refuse to support a group, they cite arguments that in fact rest on a lie. When the lie is brought to light, the now "enlightened" leader ends up shifting positions. In Nashville in 1966, for example, the African American students' campaign to desegregate lunch counters only ended after Diane Nash asked the mayor publicly whether he believed it was wrong to exclude people based only on skin color. When confronted with the naked lie, he admitted that he too believed such discrimination was wrong. That admission marked the beginning of the students' victory.

Lies in the Church

The church has, unfortunately, been complicit in perpetuating some societal lies. This is more painful and destructive for the oppressed—particularly for believers who are suffering injustice—than unjust actions by the broader society. The church's complicity manifests in its repetition of societal lies or its silence in the face of them, ignoring the Scriptures.

Another lie is that the church is for economic justice and equity when it is complicit in neo-liberal capitalism. William Connolly emphasizes, for example, the close relationship between evangelicals and capitalism: "The right leg of the evangelical movement is joined at the hip to the left leg of the capitalist juggernaut."[3] In his book *Capitalism and Christianity, American Style,* Connolly sees an "evangelical-capitalist resonance machine," where capitalists and evangelicals reach across their formal, creedal differences in the name of "existential revenge," in which participants harbor various resentments "against the human condition or your place in it. . . . It finds expression in punitive orientations toward others outside the fold: in a bellicose orientation to other faiths, states, and civilizations, in patterns of scandal and gossip, in an extreme sense of entitlement for your constituency, and in a tendency to devalue the claims and needs of other constituencies."[4]

For Connolly, counteracting the resonance machine requires a spirituality that has "affirmative orientations to being,"[5] accepting the messiness of the world in our commitment to it and confronting the lies told by the machine on a daily basis. Such a spirituality must be political and public, confronting the other big lie that spirituality is something to be kept private. As Connolly notes:

> In a different time it may have been noble to oppose the politics of human indignity in public while leaving the sources of that concern in the private realm. Today, several constituencies have left the private-public distinction behind, as they either invoke Christianity to support the politics of torture, suspension of due process, a unitary presidency, preemptive wars, and the extension of the inequality of income, job security, workers' rights, and retirement or remain silent about these issues while celebrating publicly the virtues of their faith. So it is indispensible for dissenting Christians, Jews, Muslims, and nontheists to cite publicly the sources from which they find inspiration to oppose those policies.[6]

The spirituality that undergirds faith-rooted organizing is necessarily broad-based. Everyone is needed; no one is left out. This stands in contrast to one of the most pernicious lies that the church has supported, directly and indirectly: women are less qualified and called to lead than men. The lie is particularly tragic given how much leadership women have shown in important faith-rooted movements.

Women leaders were at the forefront of the civil rights movement. Fannie Lou Hamer's leadership of Mississippi's Freedom Democratic Party in 1964 has been well chronicled. After being beaten in the Winona jail, she had a chance to speak with the jailer's wife and daughter, who had brought water and ice to the prisoners:

> And I told them, "Y'all is nice. You must be Christian people." The jailer's wife told me she tried to live a Christian life. And I told her I would like her to read two scriptures in the Bible, and I tol' her to read the 26th Chapter of Proverbs and the 26th Verse ["Whose hatred is covered by deceit, his wickedness shall be showed before the whole congregation"]. She taken it down on a paper. And then I told her to read the [17th] Chapter of Acts and the 26th Verse ["Hath made of one blood all nations of men for to dwell on all the face of the earth"]. And she taken that down. And she never did come back after then.[7]

Ella Baker, similarly, provided a much needed spark to African-American community organizing in the civil rights era. Though she was hired by the NAACP in 1941 and spent years setting up new chapters, she resigned in 1946 when she determined that the organization was more interested in raising money and increasing membership than in protests against injustice. Baker's priority was to ensure that the march toward equality continued at a steady pace. When those she worked with (including Martin Luther King Jr.) planned on letting people "catch their breath" after demonstrative action, Baker stepped in to ensure that leadership would capitalize on their gains, rather than rest on their laurels. "I don't think leadership in Montgomery," she recalls, "was prepared to capitalize . . . on [what] had become of the Montgomery situation."[8] Baker and her associates organized over one hundred African Americans, including Martin Luther King Jr., to form the Southern Christian Leadership Conference (SCLC), which would go on to organize important voter registration drives and rallies to get blacks to vote in the 1960 presidential election. Without the persistent will and drive of Baker, even stalwarts like King might have failed to capitalize on some of their biggest opportunities.

Women of faith faced adversity even within their own movements. Baker used to joke that her SCLC office was her purse and the nearest pay phone. In King's view, a woman's place was in the home; hence King had "little use for professional women."[9] When King became too much of an authoritarian figure within the SCLC and began to drift from Baker's vision, Baker was finally forced to set out on her own once again. She worked hard with young people, eventually organizing college students into what would become the Student Nonviolent Coordinating Committee (SNCC).

Baker's biggest fear was that the civil rights movement would come to resemble the black church in its propping up of charismatic figures and its exclusion of women. She opposed the kind of strong leadership she saw in figures like King, stating that "strong people don't need strong leaders."[10] She leaves us with a legacy of grassroots participation of autonomous people, in contrast to hierarchies with so-called experts directing the people. Baker's legacy is a prophetic warning against the temptation of the ego within important movements, and the imperative to empower all voices as a collective, not a hierarchy. The lie that Baker identified was that men know best. The antidote was confronting patriarchy through empowering women leaders. When we discern our own *kairos* moment we can move into a prophetic, intercultural future.

•   •   •

Dear Alina and Yehsong:

Don't just decide your issues; discern the key issues that will move justice forward in every way—the kairos issues that best reveal the deep lies used to justify injustice. Engage the people of God in exposing lies and combatting them with the truth.

5

Questions of Power and Hope

After establishing which voices to prioritize in organizing, and discerning your key issue (and its corresponding lie), you have to address the issue of power.

There is no organizing that does not face the issue of power—simply defined as the capacity to act or to influence others to act. Organizing is bringing people together to create systemic community change. Communities are most consistently affected by public decisions, decisions that affect large numbers of people, so the capacity to influence public decisions is a core strategy. Injustice results when a power imbalance allows some to consistently ensure that public decisions benefit their narrow interests while depriving or harming others.

Organizing that seeks lasting change has the explicit and implicit goal of the redistribution of power. For that reason, a context analysis always includes a power analysis. Who has the capacity and legal right to make public decisions? Who and what influences their decision-making process?

Faith-rooted organizing recognizes the need for a clear and comprehensive power analysis. However, the lens of faith changes the way that we understand power in significant ways.

A traditional power analysis assumes that there are essentially three forces that determine public power: force (including the government's

implicit capacity for force), wealth and control of resources (which includes the capacity for mass communication), and numbers. However, if
we assume that there is a God who is (a) on the side of justice and (b)
active in history, the power equation changes. There is an invisible ingre-
dient in the mix; it's possible to work in partnership with a force that
makes individual actions toward justice more powerful than the sum of
the parts.

Serpent Power and Dove Power

In Matthew 10:18, Jesus calls his disciples to be wise as serpents and innocent as doves. Serpent power is evident and measurable—it is the
power of force, wealth, social influence and numbers. There is nothing
wrong with the use of serpent power with integrity. It is in fact necessary
in a world where the kingdom of God is still a work in progress. Serpent
power is an accurate response to both the worst in people and the animal
aspects of human beings.

However, if all we use is serpent power, we have lost our unique call
and contribution—the capacity to embody the power of the dove.

Mahatma Gandhi believed that the implications of God's presence
made *ahimsa*—the power of nonviolent love—possible. Gandhi once sent
unarmed troops to take a strategic fortress in India. He placed elderly
people, children and pregnant women at the front as they rushed forward.
The soldiers initially shot into the crowd but ultimately threw down their
weapons and allowed Gandhi's forces to take the fort. It was a brilliantly
risky maneuver; Ghandi used the face of the assumed weak to resist the
power of the strong, thus revealing a deeper strength.

When we take dove power seriously, we take seriously the best in
people, the reality of the image of God in each of us and the transforming
work of the Holy Spirit. We know that power is manifested every day in
our communities in a multitude of ways. Besides the serpent powers of
position, physical force, money and numbers, we believe in the power of
prayer. We believe in the power of truth and the power of love. We believe
that there are contexts and moments in which moral authority is real,
tangible and effective.

Bishop Desmond Tutu of South Africa was threatened by the government to stop speaking out against apartheid. On one Easter morning soldiers were sent to his church. They lined the walls of the sanctuary holding loaded rifles. The congregation was frightened that Bishop Tutu would speak against apartheid and that the soldiers would start shooting. They were also frightened that he would not speak—for then the regime would have effectively won.

Bishop Tutu began bouncing on his heels and laughing, laughing uproariously, laughing like a child. The laughter was contagious. Soon everyone was laughing, even some of the soldiers. In the midst of the laughter, Bishop Tutu cried out to the soldiers "Little Brothers, you know that God is a God of justice, the God of the Exodus. You know that we are going to win. We don't want you to miss out on one moment of the celebration. Join us now! The party wouldn't be complete without you." Bishop Tutu went on to preach against apartheid and he was not shot.[1]

Bishop Tutu did not have the power of force; that was all on the side of the government. He did not have the power of wealth; no one in the cathedral that day was wealthy. He did not have the power of numbers; there were less than a thousand people present. Another bishop in another country, Archbishop Romero of El Salvador, had been assassinated under very similar circumstances. In this instance Bishop Tutu did not have serpent power; his was the power of the dove, residing in his faith, hope and love. Tutu's faith gave him the capacity for joy in all circumstances. His faith in the coming kingdom of God brought the experience of the future into the present, making it real for his audience. He did not fear for the future; he awaited it expectantly and called his listeners into it. This lack of fear allowed him to look past the guns, see the boys holding the guns, and love them. His love, faith and hope had real-world power.

Spiritual power gives people the capacity to struggle against the "powers and principalities." Rev. Charlie Sherrod tells a story about the campaign to register African American voters in Albany, Georgia:

> Albany, Georgia was segregated through and through. People were
> afraid of white folk. Black people were afraid to go downtown to

register to vote. All of them were religious. Most of them for the most part went to church consistently. You ask them if they believed in the Lord, they could talk an hour and a half on the experience they had with the Lord. And after hearing them say that so many times, we got the young people together and we talked to the older people based on their belief in the Lord. You believe in the Lord? Well why don't you go down and register? Does the Lord stop at the courthouse? Or does the belief in the Lord, the promises of the Lord go through that courthouse? Am I right or am I wrong, Ma'am? And so they had to say yes every time, every time. They had to say yes and deal with the fear they had. Cause they see me say ok come on let's go. They see me go and get smacked down, get up and go again. Get smacked down and go, and go again. And I tell them that it's based on my faith. When we're singing and praying in the church and we love the Lord, I'd come back up again. Can we take the Lord down with us to the courthouse? Or will the Lord go with us? Is the Lord scared? No, the Lord is not scared. Well, who is scared in here? There's a door, we open that door, how many of us goin' be ready to go out of that door and face the devil? And they would go.[2]

The apparent barriers to action rarely stand up to dove power. When people are reminded of the strength of their faith, their fear subsides. And when they are invited to lean into their faith, they are emboldened by God's provision. Dolores Huerta, the long-time primary organizing partner of Cesar Chavez and a Catholic lay leader, talks about how Saul Alinsky refused to support them at a key crossroads because he didn't believe it was possible to organize farmworkers.

We were sending farmworkers all over the United States of America. They're leaving Delano; they don't know where they are going to go. They have no idea, you know. They're in the car and we're saying to them, when you get to this town, to Phoenix or Salt Lake City, call and we'll tell you where you are going to be staying. Like Jesus sending out the twelve and the seventy. It was really a pilgrimage of people going across country the way that they did. And yet it worked. Farmworkers who could barely speak any English. So, I am in charge of the East Coast boycott, and a farmworker calls me, this farmworker who had never been out of his little town 2,000 miles away in New York City standing in front of a store and asking people not to buy grapes and to help him get the store to stop selling grapes, and he says Señora Huerta, they took the grapes off, they started taking the grapes off the shelves for us! I said, wonderful. What's the name of the store? He said, I don't know. I said well, look at the sign. He said, Señora, I don't know how to read. I thought oh my God, this is the power of faith.[3]

There are a number of Old and New Testament scriptures which teach that the God of justice particularly bestows alternative power on those who are least powerful in the world. Darby Ray points out that this alternative view of power is manifest in the God revealed in Jesus. The source of all power does not come to us as a "superhero" Messiah or a "superhero" God but rather as a listening God, a God who is about empathy not empire, mercy not mastery, vulnerability not violence, incarnate in a poor baby not in an earthly King. The Bible is full of the promise of power to those with little hope of attaining any standard definition of power. The meek will inherit the earth.[4]

The Dove Before the Powers and Principalities

When those with less worldly power take these promises seriously, their approach to the powerful changes. They no longer need to wrest power from the grasp of the "target." In fact, they no longer seek to "target" people, because when we see people as targets, we subconsciously seek to "shoot" them; meanwhile, a person who feels like they are being reduced to a target is less likely to compromise or be convinced.

Much as Bishop Tutu demonstrated, people with little serpent power can nevertheless minister to the powerful from a position of power and love. Jesus, a poor carpenter from Galilee, had no externally sanctioned authority "as the scribes," but his authority was regularly recognized even by those with such authority. One of the most poignant and powerful moments in Scripture is the dialogue between Jesus and Pilate: a bludgeoned and bloody prisoner in rags tells the governor who holds his life in his hands that he has no power over him—and the governor takes him seriously!

Frederick Douglass once said that "power concedes nothing without a demand. It never did and it never will."[5] Faith-rooted organizing believes that this struggle can occur within the soul of the powerful; therefore organizers can actually become allies of the powerful person who glimpses his or her connection to the rest of us. The Holy Spirit is ever at work on each of us, pulling and pushing for the victory of the best within us. Through nonviolent direct action and faith-centered moral dialogue, we can be an ally of the Spirit in its work on the soul of the person in power. We can awaken powerful people to their deeper calling and responsibility to share power.

This miracle of the movement of the Spirit in the soul of the powerful can happen in a wide variety of contexts. For example, Jack, one of the leaders of the men's ministry at a very large Southern California church, asked to meet with me (Alexia) one afternoon to confess a spiritual struggle. He had recently returned to his Christian faith and was finding that his career as the director of human resources for a multinational corporation was causing him great spiritual queasiness. He couldn't reconcile the requirements and norms of his job with his reading of Scripture. He asked for my help to create a retreat for the business leaders in his group to reflect on these issues and questions.

According to plan, Jack began the retreat with a personal confession and an invitation to confession. One of the members, Manny, then shared that as a principal in a financial management firm he was facing increasing pressure and criticism because his advice to the clients had become too "moralistic and preachy." The veiled threats of losing his job and being blacklisted had serious potential implications for his relationship with his children, as he had never been able to pull much time away from work to spend with them. His relationship with them was based on his ability to make their dreams come true financially; if he lost his job, he might lose his relationship with his kids as well.

Several other members shared their stories before the visiting speakers arrived. The first speaker, "Angelica," shared the story of her flight from El Salvador as a widow with two young children. A successful business-woman in El Salvador, she started over in the garment industry, living in a garage. She then moved up to two hotel housekeeping jobs, sharing an apartment with another family. While she was away at her night job, a member of the other family molested her daughter. At about the same time, a union organizing campaign began at her workplace. Angelica got involved and quickly become a leader, but her supervisor called her aside and said that if she didn't pull back from organizing, her hours would be sharply reduced. Angelica called her children together and told them that she was not going to stop—because she wanted not only her own children but all of the children of the workers to have mothers who earned enough to provide them with safety. She told her kids that she was responding to Jesus' call; if she lost her apartment and had to live in her car, that was his cross for her to bear. She asked her children to support her in her faith, and they agreed. Her hours were reduced, she could no longer pay her rent, and her family lived for a time in her car—until the workers won their fight for a union and their wages were raised. Her children eventually went to college and flourished.

Two months later, I came to visit the church and saw Manny. He looked relaxed and happy. He let me know that he had talked to Angelica over lunch that day, and after the retreat he went home and called his family together, asking them to support his faith as he left the firm and started a socially responsible financial management firm. The new firm was struggling, he said, and the process of rebuilding relationship with his children wasn't easy, but it was all good. Like the old hymn, he said, it was well with his soul.

The movement of the Spirit in the soul of the powerful can be intensified by a series of private and public actions. In 2002, the janitors in Southern California who worked for the largest mall management company in the world were hired by the firms who had submitted the lowest bid. That bid left little to no room for living wages, benefits or even protective equipment. The family that owned the mall company was known to be religious, so we engaged two well-known theologians from their faith tradition to write a letter calling on faithful business leaders to follow core biblical principles in their treatment and compensation of workers. Young faith leaders managed to get hundreds of clergy to sign the letter, including the leader of the family's congregation. At the same time, the director of the San Diego Interfaith Council for Worker Justice was engaged in a variety of other activities designed to call the family to moral accountability, and the workers themselves were carrying out campaign actions. Ultimately, the head of the family had a very intense conversation with his congregation's clergy; two days later, he made a commitment to a responsible bidding process that would allow for living wages and benefits.

The movement of the Spirit in the soul of the powerful can be catalyzed by the "least of these." An evangelical Christian member of the U.S. Congress refused to meet with immigration advocates for years. He had one of the strongest anti-immigration records in Congress. Then his chief of staff finally sat down with pastors and evangelical agribusiness leaders, who brought with them a young, undocumented college student. She had arrived in the United States as an infant. She declined to share her story, however, opting instead to share her faith and the stories of the people she knew who were suffering as a result of a broken immigration system. Her evident appreciation for her mother, her real love for her friends and neighbors, and her Scripture-based dream that God would bring justice spoke to the chief of staff; she stopped resorting to canned responses and engaged in a real dialogue that lasted for more than an hour.

The movement of the Spirit in the soul of the powerful can be stirred up by an act of persistent faith. When security officers at multiple properties owned by a Southern California real estate firm protested their very low wages, lack of benefits and lack of training, the vice president of the firm stood by watching quietly until the buzz among the workers alerted James M. Lawson Jr. to his presence. Lawson walked over and introduced himself. And then, standing close and looking in his eyes, he spoke directly: in his soul, Lawson knew, this vice president did not want the security officers protecting his building to be unable to afford rent and adequate food or medical care for their children. The vice president responded with reasons and excuses, but Rev. Lawson continued to speak to his soul: he knew that this man did not want his officers to risk their lives without adequate equipment or training. The firm ultimately changed its unjust practices.

Dove power works on a macro and micro level, on big canvasses and in intimate interactions. Dorothy Day, the cofounder of the Catholic Worker movement, was once being given a tour of a mental hospital when she was told about a man who lived alone in a padded room because of his violent impulses. She demanded to be taken into the room. At first, as she stood in the middle of the room holding out her hand to him, he alternated between screaming rage and sudden withdrawals into shaking terror. But he didn't hit her, and she didn't move. After a while his circling grew calmer and he finally came forward and took her hand. He then fell into her arms weeping.

Shortly after I (Alexia) first read that story, when I was working for the Berkeley Emergency Food Project, a well-known homeless man called Gypsy came into my office wanting to speak with me privately. When I closed the door, he pulled out a sawed-off shotgun and told me that he was going to go shoot his wife because she had cheated on him. I stood frozen, knowing that I could not get to the phone to call the police before he could shoot me. I decided instead to go the dove route.

I sat down with Gypsy and talked with him, reminding him of the flame of love in his heart that would be destroyed by the darkness if he shot his wife. I reminded him of all that we loved about him and all we would miss if the darkness won. I reminded him of Jesus' invisible arms around him as we spoke. Ultimately, he handed me the gun and wept while I held his hands.

The power of the dove is not always this successful of course; the risk is real. And in any case, it requires immense courage. Nelson and Joyce Johnson direct the Beloved Community Center in Greensboro, North Carolina, where a famous massacre occurred during the days of the civil rights marches. With the police standing by, Ku Klux Klan members shot into a nonviolent procession, killing and wounding a number of people, including Nelson, who had been one of the march organizers. He eventually became a Christian and then a pastor, but he could not forget the massacre; he felt that it was a spiritual infection in the "body" of that community. He decided to establish a Truth and Reconciliation Commission, similar to the one in post-Apartheid South Africa, to bring healing through confession and forgiveness.

Organizers decided to kick off the commission with a nonviolent march when they heard that the Klan was planning a counterprotest. Nelson called the local head of the Klan and asked if he could come and speak with him. The head of the Klan laughed and instructed him to come to a gas station. There he was blindfolded and taken to the apartment building that housed the Klan's offices. Nelson was taken upstairs and frisked to ensure that he had no weapon, at which point he was allowed to talk to the man in charge. Nelson laid out his case for reconciliation and healing in the name of Christ. By the end of the meeting, the man had agreed not to do the counterprotest, but his final words were chilling. "Boy," he said to Nelson, "look out that window." There was a man in the window of the building opposite with a rifle pointed at him. The Klan leader continued: "If you had come in here with a gun, you would have been dead. The reason why I said yes to your proposal was because you had the balls to come in here unarmed. That's real faith."[6]

The power of the dove may be gentle but it is not soft; it requires the ultimate in courageous faith—and not just from those in the line of fire. Sometimes it takes as much or even more courage and faith to support your loved ones in their commitment to nonviolent action than it does to risk your own life. Joyce, for example, knew what her husband was planning to do when he left the house, and she knew there was a good chance that she would never see him again. "I had to trust God enough to let him go, to not try to stop him," she says. "It was one of the hardest tasks that I was ever given."[7]

Power Mapping

An essential organizing tool for both serpent power and dove power is power mapping, a topography of individual, corporate and institutional power. Power mapping is a way of identifying who has various kinds and levels of decision-making power in our communities—as well as who influences those decision-makers.

Inexperienced organizers and new organizations often make the mistake of focusing their energy and efforts on people who don't actually have the power to fix the problem. A city council member, for example, usually has little to no control over the school system, which is run by the school board. Some decisions are made by federal officials through those structures; others are made by decision makers at the state level. These structures are not completely separate and immovable, further cluttering the landscape. A variety of states, for example, have been taking the federal issue of immigration into their own hands, with varying results. A group utilizes its resources for maximum benefit when it knows who makes which decisions and how best to influence them.

Faith-rooted organizing also uses power-mapping. It is a necessary aspect of being "wise as serpents." However, after creating a power map, we then create an "alternative power map," to recognize other, spiritual powers in play.

This alternative power map first names the special power possessed by the "last and least," effectively inverting the perceived power structure. Moving the people on the bottom of a power chart to the top of the chart can change the energy of a roomful of people who are used to seeing themselves as powerless.

After naming the power of the last and least, we then look at spiritual lines of influence. What religious faith do powerful people espouse? How are the last and least connected to more powerful congregations; can we talk to them as peers because of the common sacred ground on which we stand? Can we mobilize the clergy of the powerful to stand for and with us? Taking seriously that the powerful are often believers, what do we notice that they are called to? Who do they care for? What connections can we draw between their passions and concerns and ours?

To advocate, in the context of faith-rooted organizing, is to minister to leaders. When a leader is a believer, this is a form of discipleship. When a leader is not a believer, it is a form of evangelism. Often both discipleship and evangelism are taking place in the same act of advocacy: when

Dr. King spoke the words of the prophet Isaiah in his famous "I Have a Dream" speech, he moved a nation—believers and unbelievers alike.

Unreasonable Hope

Our religious traditions affect not only how we believe that change occurs but whether we believe it can occur. As Corey Beals says, "The hardest continual quality to maintain is hope."[8] However, as the Muslim students at CLUE often told us, "Hope is the defining characteristic of a person of faith."

Hope begins with seeing possibilities. Theologian Sharon Welch takes her students on "beauty walks" where they explore a "blighted" area and seek to identify all the signs of beauty, love, creativity—every positive good that others might miss. God is, after all, in every place of poverty, degradation, oppression and anguish, long before helpful outsiders arrive. God is doing small miracles constantly, loving people with power and passion more than we could ever imagine or accomplish.

Because of the powerful love of God, people of God envision and trust in possibilities that others see as foolish or insane. This allows us to choose and continue struggles that are not quickly or easily winnable, if we perceive that the cause is righteous and therefore supported by divine power. This does not excuse us from being strategic; advocating for faith is not the same as endorsing blind faith. It does, however, enable and push us to move forward on the basis of the value of a cause even if we cannot see all the steps necessary to succeed. It enables us to take the long view, to fight for a cause that it critically important even if we will not win for generations.

CLUE's vision of the horizon allows it to work in a coalition for economic justice in which low-wage workers themselves lead. The strategies of those who are in solidarity with the workers are dependent on and subject to the workers' strategies more so than their own expertise, so that the workers experience the fullness of their power in the process. As a result of their faith in the long arc of God's work, CLUE also can take on multi-year struggles to hold multinational corporations accountable. From 2004-2006, for example, hotel workers across the country took on the whole luxury hotel industry. The ownership of luxury hotels had become increasingly consolidated into a few chains, which were themselves owned by multinational, multi-industry conglomerates. Hotel workers in any given local area had little to no hope of a dialogue with the owners of these conglomerates. Their interests, needs and concerns would be irrelevant, their leverage nonexistent. The little Hotel and Restaurant Employees Union decided that their only chance was to align their contract termination dates across multiple cities. If hotel housekeepers in large urban centers across the country could fight for a contract at the same time, they could leverage their power to have a large enough voice to mandate a dialogue.

At the beginning of their struggle, the general wisdom was that this was a hopeless mission. Why would these multinational employers ever agree to align the termination dates of the contracts? Why would they give their primarily low-income, immigrant, female workers of color the leverage to demand a dialogue? But the struggle looked different through the eyes of faith. Faith leaders who knew the struggle of the hotel housekeepers for basic rights, dignity and the capacity to sustain their families believed that this struggle was both necessary and possible.

Hotel employees in ten cities worked intimately and doggedly with community and faith allies for two years to build public support for the workers' goal. One afternoon at the Sheraton Hotel in Los Angeles, for example, the Methodist bishop spoke at a rally in front of the hotel (promising housekeepers who cared for her on her frequent travels that she would care for them), while clergy from all denominations entered quietly into the hotel and took up positions in different locations. A rabbi sat by the pool, a Catholic priest in the bar, an evangelical pastor in the Café, an imam in the lobby, and so on. On cue they all stood up and began to preach about economic justice and the plight of the hotel workers and their families.

The clergy expected to be thrown out immediately, but twenty minutes later the hotel management was still trying to decide what to do. As the faith leaders joined a procession out of the hotel, guests and media alike discussed the struggle for fair wages and just working conditions.

Against all apparent odds, the hotel workers aligned all their contracts and were able to keep their union alive. To believe that low-wage, pri-

marily immigrant workers of color could convince multinational corporations to allow them to negotiate as a national block was an act of radical
hope, like David facing Goliath. The small defeated the great through the
power of righteousness.

David and Goliath struggles seem impossible, but in the biblical narrative David wins—and when people of faith and the poor stand on that
promise of possibility, David often continues to win. Indeed, as one of the
architects of the 1990s Justice for Janitors campaign, Jono Shaefer, says,
"We always win; it is only a matter of time."[9]

•   •   •

Dear Alina and Yehsong:

*The world will tell you that the only real power is serpent power. Don't
believe it. Engage the people in mastering the appropriate use of serpent
and dove power, in the faith that it all belongs to the one power who
creates and sustains the whole earth.*

And remember: the last will be first and the first will be last.

6

The Gift of Christ-Centered Community

The scriptural vision of justice within shalom calls us to the *practice of intelligent love*. We have to respond to the needs of our neighbors as effectively as possible. Moving beyond charity to community development is an act of intelligent love. In the words of the parable, if you give a woman a fish, she eats a meal; if you teach her how to fish, she eats for a lifetime. If, however, someone has built a wall around the pond or polluted the water, she also needs to know who to meet with in order to get the pond cleaned up and the wall taken down. This requires advocacy—the process of influencing public decision-makers to make decisions that benefit the community.

Biblically Based Public Policy Advocacy
The Scriptures support advocacy when it comes to public policy. Romans 13 teaches that governments have a divine purpose to ensure the well-being of their society. And in the Hebrew Scriptures, the King is often exhorted to ensure justice for the poor and to care for the widow, the orphan and the stranger. Psalm 72 is an excellent example. The psalmist asks God to ensure that the king judges the poor with justice—that he defends the cause of the poor, gives deliverance to the needy, crushes the

oppressor, has pity on the weak and saves the lives of the needy, particularly children. This vision of the call of government goes well beyond national defense.

In a monarchy, the king has the power and responsibility to fulfill this command. In a democracy, we all have the power—and the corresponding responsibility. Democracy does not function effectively unless the people participate as active citizens—which is why we call our legislators "representatives." As surely as children's behavior reflects on their families, our legislators' behavior reflects on our communities. If our representatives do not fulfill God's purpose for government, we are the ones to be held responsible. A democratic system gives us the opportunity to call on our representatives to enact policies that will fulfill the divine purpose of government. This is good stewardship of the gift of democracy.

Movements for change utilize a complex set of strategies, which include a wide variety of ways we can communicate with and influence policymakers—from letters, internet blitzes, telephone calls, precinct walking, legislative visits and testimonies at hearings, to direct public actions, media outreach and civil disobedience. Policymakers are more likely to fulfill the biblical mandate to ensure justice if community members effectively call them to accountability. So building voice and power for community members is a necessary goal of organizing.

However, in faith-rooted organizing our goals are not instrumental but holistic. We are not just seeking to meet immediate needs or solve present problems. We are not about winning power for its own sake. Power is a means to an end. We must always ask "Power for what purpose?" Our rich sources of revelation provide us with information about the kind of community and society that is our proper common destination.

The realization of God's dreams will take more than just the church. Christians need to work collaboratively with other faiths and a broader coalition of community groups—including labor unions, community groups, and political groups—to hold government accountable to just policies. Churches, government and a variety of sectors in society will be called and gifted to do their part for the common good.

Economic Advocacy

While organizing focuses on public, governmental decisions, corporate decisions also impact large numbers of people and so merit attention. Small businesses, like private individuals or families, have limited capacity to impact public life, but corporations that hire thousands of people can affect both the lives of their employees and the well-being of whole communities. Corporations have direct impact on the environment, and they influence wage and price structures for hosts of smaller businesses. They also have public power in a less direct form; they buy an inordinate percentage of media space and time, as well as funding innumerable precinct walkers for the politicians they support (particularly since the decision in the Supreme Court case *Citizens United* v. *Federal Elections Commission* removed multiple restrictions on corporate contributions to the political process).

While corporations have inordinate serpent power, there are ways that an organized group of people can impact corporate decisions. Unions, for example, allow workers to have a collective voice and to bargain as a group. Customers can use purchasing power to impact businesses that need their support. Shareholders have a voice in publicly traded companies and can combine their votes in shareholders' meetings to achieve their ends.

Faith-rooted advocacy takes on economic and political decision-makers alike. It thrives in coalitions with voluntary associations (often referred to globally as civil society), the press and other entities that have political and economic influence. All these are important potential partners for the faith community.

Secular Partnerships—In the World, Not of the World

A Latin American representative at the World Council of Churches made a provocative prediction at a conference in Northern California:

> Over the next twenty years, we will see increasing political democracy and increasing economic consolidation of power, economic tyranny. People will seem more free but they will feel less

free. The schizophrenic contract between the two will create disorientation and fear. This fear will drive people towards simplistic solutions and demigods. False religion will distract people and obscure the reality they face. True religion will reveal it.[1]

The faith community cannot stand alone in the struggle for justice. We are most effective when we work collaboratively, partnering with different sectors and groups that share our fundamental aims, and collaborating with trusted secular partners—organizations that themselves are often filled with people of faith who look to us for solidarity and, at times, spiritual guidance.

In order to be biblically faithful, our partnerships must conform to certain core values. While we obviously cannot participate in actions that violate core tenets of our faith, in the daily give and take of collaboration, we are called to partner in a way that reflects the spirit of Jesus Christ,

Who, being in very nature God,
did not consider equality with God something to be used to his
    own advantage;
rather, he made himself nothing
by taking the very nature of a servant,
being made in human likeness.
And being found in appearance as a man,
he humbled himself
by becoming obedient to death—
    even death on a cross! (Philippians 2:6-8)

As Jesus humbled himself, becoming human so he could serve humanity, Christians need to humble themselves and serve others with empathetic hearts. Darby Ray says, "We need to be motivated by empathy, not empire; mercy, not mastery; vulnerability, not violence. Humility comes from *humus*, the word for earth, becoming earth, becoming incarnate."[2] We need to be known for our humility, respecting the contribution of each sector and the special role of the poor.

When broad coalitions hesitate to involve faith leaders, and particularly evangelical Christians, it's often because they have experienced us as arrogant—identifying God's absolute truth and our complete correctness, and demanding an extra measure of control.

Even though there are respectable intellectual grounds for belief, it is not possible to provide iron-clad proof; that's why religious conviction, let alone discipleship, requires an act of faith. To be truly humble is in itself an act of profound faith and a powerful witness to a loving God.

Many years ago, the British Broadcasting Corporation held a series of debates between faith leaders and atheists. It was agonizing to watch; the more fiercely the eminent apologists argued, the less personally appealing they became. But then the show featured East Indian Jesuit Brother Anthony de Mello. Brother Anthony was comfortable with not being able to answer some of the questions of his opponents. Instead he seemed to be primarily interested in them as people, asking them why they believed in their convictions, wanting to know the events that had passed in their lives which had led them to that point. He was compassionate about the pain and loneliness that often accompany atheism.

After a while, all of Brother Anthony's opponents fell silent. When the moderator asked why they were quiet, the ringleader replied that it was impossible to argue against the existence of God with a man who is sitting in God's presence.

On a practical level, to be humble in a coalition sets an example that can save a collaborative effort from ego-driven conflict and competition. From 2009 to 2011, there were multiple attempts at organizing a regional coalition for child protection in Eastern Europe. Each failed when the members of the coalition perceived that the organizers were using the coalition for their own organizational advantage. Then the staff of World Vision in Romania decided to live their Christian faith by not putting their logo or name on the coalition that they devoted staff time to organize. The coalition has survived and thrived, changing law and enforcement policies throughout the region for the well-being of children.

To be humble in relationship to the perspective of the poor can call a larger coalition to truly respect its poorer members rather than patronizing or exploiting them. Humility entails being open to God's spirit moving in innovative ways through all of the people in the coalition, especially the poor and marginalized. When CLUE Los Angeles works on economic justice campaigns, they take their cues in core strategic questions from the low-wage worker leaders with the most risk and investment in the campaign.

Even while we are committed to humility, however, we are also clear about the call to prophetic boldness. Clergy and congregational leaders have unique roles to play and contributions to make. We have access to specialized strategies that utilize our particular gifts and resources to advance the common cause. We lose our unique power when we do the same activities in the same way, using the same talking points as other sectors. Faith leaders must approach our task embracing the paradoxical integration of prophetic boldness and authentic humility. This is at the core of the dance of solidarity.

Before we can discuss the specific activities that are uniquely suited to people of faith, we need to start by recognizing the context in which faith-rooted organizing is exercised and nurtured—the congregation or faith community. When Saul Alinsky began his organizing work, he was somewhat suspicious of congregations, worried that their allegiance to hierarchical institutions would compromise organizing strategies and weaken commitment. Over time, however, Alinsky affiliates and offshoots have recognized that congregations are a reliable source for encountering community members and a natural base for developing leaders. Through congregations, organizations have regular access to an organizing group of residents and allies. Particularly in low-income communities where many institutions are transitory, congregations have often been the backbone of any effort to bring people together to address common problems.

Faith-based organizing views congregations as a critically important asset because of their constituency. However, congregations have far more to contribute than just an accessible constituency.

The Gift of Christ-Centered Community

Organizing is exhausting. The forces of injustice are often ruthless and so well-funded that they have replacements ready to go each time a foot soldier tires. In many countries (and in certain times and places in the United States), organizers face the regular threat of violence. There are never enough resources or staff; organizers must, as the White Queen said in *Alice in Wonderland,* do three impossible things before breakfast.

Organizing culture, particularly in the United States, is often brutal in its constant demand to put the cause above all other aspects of life. This results in organizations which resemble the military in their reliance on young, relatively inexperienced recruits, who leave the field after a few years of work. While organizers may build relationships that go beyond work, the bottom line assumption is that they are together to do a job. Their value to the organization comes from their efforts and achievements.

Congregations are unique in the U.S. movement for justice in that they maintain two simultaneous purposes—working to change the broader community while also becoming a model community. Congregations and other faith communities are focused not only on achieving an objective mission in the outside world but also on the personal growth of every individual and the task of caring for one another. These are understood as intrinsically worthy goals. People come to congregations to be healed from their wounds and sustained in their daily lives and work. While congregations often demand a high level of sacrifice, they are intentionally formed to be holistic communities.

Love. When the church is fulfilling its call, people in faith communities are regularly renewed by love. And when a faith community teaches the "theology from below," its members are also inspired and equipped to be the body of Jesus Christ, broken in and for the world. Members are energized by the deep bond of love that unites Jesus and the church; they challenge one another, the larger religious institutions and the whole society to live under God's reign of love and justice. Congregational practices that encourage the rhythm of contemplation and action, sabbath rest and committed discipleship also help to build healthy individuals and relationships. Practices such as repentance, honest confession, forgiveness and reconciliation also help deepen and sustain healthy relationships over time.

Family. In addition, congregations are full of families rooted in faith traditions which view the family as the core building block of society.

Congregations have historically devoted significant resources and activities to caring for and supporting families. Meanwhile, as Alinsky writes, "the marriage record of organizers is with rare exception disastrous."[3] The children of successful organizers often have little connection with (and even some resentment for) their parents. Congregations that take their jobs seriously as nurturers of kingdom communities help families, including children, to participate on multiple levels in God's work of justice, and make space for their needs.

Liturgies. When children are involved, organizing becomes more likely to respect and care for the child in each of us. Spiritual renewal often comes from shared lamentation and celebration; children need activities that are colorful and emotionally vibrant. It is no accident that ancient liturgies are packed with activities that appeal to all the senses and provoke a variety of emotions. Activities such as Seder meals ritually celebrating the liberation of Hebrew slaves from Egypt (in the Jewish community) or *posadas* (a Hispanic ritual in which processions reenact Mary and Joseph's search for a place to give birth) awaken hearts and minds to a re-energizing and sustaining message.

Music. Recent studies tell us that music has measurable healing properties. As an ongoing part of congregational life, we see the power of music to provide healing and hope. Paul Gilroy argues in *The Black Atlantic* that music was integral to identity formation among the African diaspora because it could express the horror of the Middle Passage and slavery through primarily nonrepresentational forms.[4] From the Underground Railroad for escaping slaves to the civil rights movement, music has fueled the struggle for justice. The spirituals and the blues were a deep river of strength amidst weakness, triumph amidst tragedy and hope amidst despair.[5]

Prayer. Prayer—the lifeblood of spiritual communities—nurtures and heals us while giving us real power to carry out our mission. Prayer is not a strategy; it is a way of life. However, believers agree that prayer has power, and it is no shame to use our power for God's purposes. In fact, it is our calling to do so.

Most congregational prayers for leaders are perfunctory—a line or two in a worship service. In faith-rooted organizing, we have learned on the ground that prayer is as effective in the public arena as it is in the private arena. The San Diego Interfaith Committee for Worker Justice (ICWJ) was part of a broad coalition working to pass living wage legislation. The coalition attended city council meetings every week and used the public commentary period to raise its concerns. As is common practice, the coalition carefully crafted talking points to ensure that the comments all communicated a common and clear message. But the San Diego ICWJ decided that they needed to participate in an alternative, faith-rooted way. So every one of their leaders that approached the podium used their time (one to three minutes) to pray. They prayed for the poor, for the community and for the city council. They prayed in whatever way they felt called to pray. When the legislation passed, a journalist asked a conservative council member why he had voted for the living wage. He responded that he could not take being prayed for one more week. He had armed himself against the talking points, but he had no armor against the prayer. The prayer reached his heart.

A few years later, a coalition of congregations named Amos in Cincinnati, Ohio (utilizing a hybrid of faith-rooted and more traditional organizing), was trying to pass legislation that would increase the availability of municipal jobs to ex-offenders. They were aware that this issue had major racial implications; African Americans in Cincinnati were more likely to go to prison for a crime in situations when others would be given less severe penalties. Amos assigned two to three congregations to pray fervently and regularly for each city council member. They let city council members know that they were being prayed for; in fact, they sometimes prayed with them and even over them. The struggle to pass the legislation had been long and hard, but when the extra element of prayer was added, the legislation passed.

Fasting. Jesus said that certain demons could only be expelled with prayer and fasting. Cesar Chavez utilized fasting and prayer for multiple purposes. According to Dolores Huerta, Cesar fasted when farmworkers were murdered while on strike. He encouraged the whole farmworker community to join him, trusting that fasting and prayer would help them to remain strong in their faith and resolve. He would fast regularly for three days or for seven days when important negotiations were coming up for the sake of clarity in hearing God's voice. He was also known for his extended fasts, which helped preserve the nonviolent commitment of his movement and, in 1972, served to take the hatred out of the hearts of the growers in Arizona. Thanks in part to his extended fast there, a law was defeated that would have made it illegal for farmworkers to strike or boycott.

In 1999 Maria Elena Durazo, the deeply faithful president of Local 11 of the Hotel Employees and Restaurant Employees Union was fighting to save the jobs of unionized food workers at the University of Southern California. She prayed and fasted for a month and was ultimately joined by hundreds of workers, students and faculty. The university changed its policies, and the jobs were saved. I (Alexia) have been part of many campaigns since then where workers have fasted and prayed publicly for days, sleeping in encampments in front of their corporate employers, joined by clergy and congregational leaders. These extended fasts have served to strengthen the workers and build community support, even when they do not succeed in moving the hearts of the mighty.

Cesar never wanted to call a fast a hunger strike because he never wanted it to be coercive; instead, he saw it as an offering to God. Fasting helps faith-rooted organizers surrender their souls to God, while also inspiring the movement to press on in the struggle.

Confession and Repentance

Two of the fruits of prayer and fasting are confession and repentance. Evangelicals have always emphasized personal confession of sin, but are now waking up to realize that confession has a public dimension.

As we seek to be prophetic faith-rooted organizers today we need to confess our sins both personally and collectively. For theologian Dietrich Bonhoeffer, confession is the conscious identification of the sin that a person and community struggles with, while repentance is an embodiment of the confession in public. Inspired by Bonhoeffer, theologian Jennifer M. McBride argues that confession unto repentance offers a concrete form of public witness.[6] Confession of sin correlates to prayer, while repentant action in the public square correlates to doing justice.

A passion for justice energized Bonhoeffer's life and witness. When offered a prestigious professorship at Union Theological Seminary in New York, Bonhoeffer instead returned to Germany to join the Confessing Church's struggle against Adolf Hitler. When he learned of the mass executions of Jews, Bonhoeffer knew he needed to act. The Nazi authorities eventually uncovered his participation in a conspiracy to assassinate Hitler, and he was arrested and executed. It is in his correspondence from prison that Bonhoeffer begins to speak of the *secret discipline*.[7]

Bonhoeffer had witnessed many German churches supporting the Nazi regime and demonstrating a virulent anti-Semitism, even seeking to sever Christianity from its Jewish roots.[8] Indignant about the church's complicity with Nazism, Bonhoeffer offered the secret discipline as a path for the materialization of a mystical-prophetic church. Renouncing the way Christian rhetoric was deployed for political power, Bonhoeffer argued that the church should reclaim its public witness through contemplative activism.

The ancient church's practice of "the arcane discipline"—concealing liturgical practices from public view—ensured that the mysteries of Christian faith would not be misunderstood by those who were not baptized and catechized members of the church, a concern based on Jesus' teaching: "Do not give dogs what is sacred; do not throw your pearls to pigs. If you do, they may trample them under their feet, and then turn and tear you to pieces" (Matthew 7:6). Bonhoeffer thought the Christian's prayer life and the church's liturgical life should be directed to God in secret (Matthew 6:6), while its public witness—the work of righteous action, or doing justice—should manifest itself in compassionate and wise acts of social transformation. As Charles Marsh points out, the practice of the secret discipline would be accompanied by "sweeping ecclesial reforms. The Church would give away all its assets and serve the world anonymously, refusing to call attention to itself."[9] This meant, for Bonhoeffer, that "all Christian thinking, speaking, and action shall be limited to prayer and righteous action. . . . The time for words is over."[10] People recognize our convictions through our actions more than our words.

Confession and repentance were integral to the church fulfilling its mission, according to Bonhoeffer. By wearing the "rags of confession and repentance," the church can bear witness to the injustices of the world.[11]

> In earlier times the church could preach that a person must first become a sinner, like the publican and the harlot, before he could know and find Christ, but we in our time must rather say that before a person can know and find Christ he must first become righteous like those who strive and who suffer for the sake of justice, truth, and humanity.[12]

In the United States this means that the church's ministry of justice should be the test of its claim to profess faith in the crucified Christ. Creative, repentant activity in the public square is a vital part of the church's mission to love God, love our neighbor and care for the community of creation. One Ash Wednesday, a group of hotel workers in Glendale, California, wanted to go to church and participate in the ancient ritual of repentance. Three lines formed in front of the hotel—a line for the imposition of ashes (for Christian workers from liturgical traditions), a line for the laying on of hands and prayer (for evangelical and other nonliturgical workers) and a line led by a rabbi for the blessing for *chuvah* (the Jewish concept of repentance). The workers invited their managers to participate in the repentance ritual, but the managers declined to join them, Nevertheless, the workers were strengthened by the experience, attaining the spirit of humility and boldness that would sustain them in a years-long struggle for union representation that was ultimately victorious.

Moral Dialogue

The members of a church do not share a common self-interest in the normative sense. The unity of a church does not depend on nor require ethnic, cultural, class or political homogeneity. Public policies that will benefit certain members of the church may result in losses for others. Their common ground is their common commitment to seek and obey God's will. They come together to discover that which is true and good, in the faith that this will ultimately benefit the whole creation even if it requires sacrifice in the meantime.

Moral authority is at its most powerful when it is wielded together by people who are the most vulnerable in intimate solidarity with those who could easily walk away. This prophetic partnership where communities of privilege relinquish power to follow and accompany the most affected communities is why the civil rights movement and the Central American Sanctuary Movement were so vibrant. When such people in partnership approach a public decision-maker, they are not entering into a negotiation of their interests with his or hers. Rather they are calling on that public leader to enter with them into the process of truly discerning the common good. Standing on the ground of their own repentance of all that would get in the way of the best outcome for their community, they call their leaders similarly to repent and to live courageously and self-sacrificially in the world.

Before such different parties can come together to exercise moral authority, however, they must first discern a common moral ground. Congregations—particularly when they feel connected to and trust each other because of their common sacred ground—are among the best (and often the only available) contexts in our society in which people can enter into moral dialogue across all of the lines that otherwise divide us. Through Bible studies, prayer groups and small groups, churches offer multiple opportunities for the cultivation of moral conversation with deep respect conveyed through a sensitive, empathetic listening to the Other.

The capacity of congregations and other religious communions to come together across a very broad spectrum is critically important at times when our social and political divisions keep us from working together. It is even more important when powerful corporate, political and institutional leaders seek to protect their power and their interests by encouraging and manipulating these divisions. Bipartisan efforts to attain the reform of a badly broken immigration system, for example, stumbled for years on the perception of the issue as a partisan cause.

In 2004 Walmart intended to build a supercenter in Inglewood, a primarily low-income and minority city in Los Angeles County. Los Angeles

Alliance for a New Economy (LAANE), an organization dedicated to research, public policy and community organizing for economic justice, led a campaign to educate the community about the impact of this proposed development on small business and grocery stores that were providing Inglewood with living wages and health benefits. LAANE's efforts were so successful that Walmart found itself unable to pass its initiative through several city commissions.

Walmart moved to the ballot, proposing legislation that would circumvent all community processes to allow the development to go forward. While LAANE leaders went door to door to bring their case to residents, Walmart paid for commercials on television, and also hired young people from the community to go door to door as well. The arguments put forward by Walmart were often unfounded; for example, they touted the quality of their health insurance program, even though new employees at Walmart were routinely taught to apply for the California version of Medicaid. The confusion caused by the multiple competing messages about Walmart's proposal threatened to keep residents from going to the polls.

When CLUE became involved in the struggle, the churches began to organize moral dialogues about Walmart. The Friday before the Walmart proposal went before the electorate, polls showed that it would win by a 10 percent margin. But that weekend, an estimated twenty thousand people discussed the Walmart proposal in congregation-based, honest explorations of the true impact and moral implications of the proposal. On Tuesday, Walmart lost 63 percent to 37 percent. While we cannot underestimate the hard work of LAANE and other community volunteers in precinct walking and phone-banking over that long weekend, the capacity of congregations to provide contexts for moral dialogue was a significant gift to the movement for justice and the ultimate victory in that campaign.

The practice of faith-rooted public policy advocacy based in moral authority has given birth to an alternative structure of communication with legislative representatives. Traditionally, a group would come to agreement on a particular policy, which the legislator might simply poke holes in. Under this new paradigm a group merely needs to come to agreement on the core principles that must be incorporated into any policy. The group can then demand that the policymaker create a policy that will put the principles into practice. This allows for a much broader coalition while stopping legislators from hiding behind the weaknesses in a particular policy.

The newly formed national Evangelical Immigration Table, for example, has members ranging from Richard Land of the Southern Baptist Convention to Gabriel Salguero from the new National Latino Evangelical Coalition. While these different leaders might disagree on specific policies, because of their commitment to unite around scriptural principles, they can advocate powerfully together for a just immigration system. The Table's core campaign, the "I Was a Stranger Challenge," calls on pastors to invite their legislators to join them in forty days studying forty scriptures related to immigration. In the first six weeks of the campaign, over 60,000 Christians took the challenge. The powerful Word of God shifts the orientation of believing legislators from hostility to hospitality. After that fundamental orientation changes, other immigration advocates carry on the conversation about specific policies.

The Circle of Care

The greatest concentration of warehouses in the world is in the Inland Empire in Southern California, where 100,000 warehouse workers labor, most through temporary agencies for minimum wage and no health benefits. These workers can lose their jobs in a moment if they stand up for their rights. CLUE's Inland Empire affiliate worked with Warehouse Workers United (a worker association organized by Change to Win) to organize a resource fair and produce a handbook of emergency resources available to workers and their families. Many of those resources were provided by churches. This circle of care provided the support that some workers needed in order to begin to advocate for themselves and each other.

Among other things, congregations are known for simple acts of caring. Members bring meals to the ill and grieving, and operate food pantries for the hungry. Some congregations find jobs for unemployed members and help one another with rent payments. More sophisticated congregations provide child care and job training services; some even develop affordable housing projects.

Members of healthy congregations that engage in justice movements learn how to work as a team, taking turns on the front line, caring for each other's families and making room for the gifts and interests of each as needed. While this kind of caring is not sufficient in itself to address systemic problems and barriers, these circles of care offer a great service to the movement for justice.

The Circle of Care can go further than just giving charity. When mobilized through faith-rooted organizing, it can materialize justice in workplaces and communities. In Santa Monica, California, for example, a housekeeper in a luxury hotel who had established an excellent work record for many years was fired as a result of her advocacy for fair health benefits in the workplace. A network of CLUE congregations stepped in to help. Besides providing emergency assistance, their care for the housekeeper also compelled many of them to call the manager. After a day of over three hundred calls by congregation members and community residents, the manager reinstated the worker's job. The rest of the workers, who had been frightened and intimidated by her firing, were inspired and strengthened in their struggle.

The Circle of Care can also be expressed symbolically and still experienced as a direct support and gift. In the New Sanctuary Movement, every immigrant family entering into a sanctuary arrangement with a network of congregations participated in a ceremony in which the family was surrounded by members and leaders of the sponsoring congregations. They were symbolically welcomed into the protection of the church. I will always remember the surprised and happy look in the eyes of a six-year-old child as the diverse group of faith leaders surrounded her and her mother with warmth and love.

The Circle of Care is rooted in hospitality, which is a necessary virtue when cultivating openness to the Other. True worship, in fact, involves hospitality—living out the vision of God through inviting all those who are excluded by the inhospitableness of the world into our homes and houses of faith.

Hospitality

Hospitality is at the heart of the Christian life (Romans 12:13). Abraham shows us what hospitality looks like, when under the oaks of Mamre he is visited by three strangers (Genesis 18). He invites them into his tent, breaking bread with them and serving a choice lamb. Breaking bread in the ancient Near East was the height of hospitality. When tribes were at war with each other, if someone walked into a member of the warring tribe's home and ate some bread, the host family was bound to care for them. In showing hospitality to the three strangers, Abraham embodies love supreme.

Hospitality is risky business. Are we willing to invite the stranger into our homes, no matter what the outcome or cost? A stranger may bring danger, even death. The stranger may rape or murder you, may steal your inheritance, and may create problems in your neighborhood. And yet, even given the ever-present danger associated with it, God's constant call to Israel is to offer hospitality to the stranger.

The call to be hospitable to our neighbors is rooted in the nature of our hospitable God. French philosopher Jacques Derrida argues that God is pure hospitality. Even speaking about God is an expression of a radical, impossible-made-possible form of hospitality. This is not impossibility as in a square circle but the emergence of a possibility that we could never foresee ahead of time, something that only can be comprehended in retrospect.

Why is hospitality, however, so "impossible"? One thing Derrida emphasizes over and over in his work is what he calls "undecideability," the inability to know in advance how a situation will turn out. Every decision, including the decision to extend hospitality to an Other, is the result of a process, an exposure to an indiscernible risk. The impossibility of the risk is that there is no way to know what is on the other side of the door. We are called to be hospitable, but we never know how that hospitality will play out. We can never know if an axe-murderer or an angel knocks on our door in the middle of the night. This does not mean that every decision is groundless, but it does mean that hospitality, like any true ethical action, asks us to leap into the realm of the impossible-made-possible with God.

In the Gospel accounts, the angel Gabriel visits Mary, and the Lord imparts to Mary a miracle that is the impossible made possible by Mary's yes to God (Luke 1:27-38). Almost all of the Hebrew prophets call for hospitality to replace empty worship and malicious feasts in the house of God. Isaiah juxtaposes the worship of God and hospitality for the poor and stranger in this way:

> Is not this the kind of fasting that I have chosen:
> to loose the chains of injustice,
>   and untie the cords of the yoke,
> to set the oppressed free,
>   and break every yoke?
> Is it not to share your food with the hungry,
>   and to provide the poor wanderer with shelter—
> when you see the naked, to clothe them,
>   and not to turn away from your own flesh and blood?
> Then your light will break forth like the dawn,
>   and your healing will quickly appear;
> then your righteousness will go before you,
>   and the glory of the LORD will be your rear guard.
> Then you will call, and the LORD will answer;
>   you will cry for help, and he will say: Here am I. (Isaiah 58:6-9;
>   cf. Isaiah 1:12-17; Amos 2:6-7; 5:21-24)

The fasting that God calls for opens our hearts, homes and houses of worship to all people, especially the oppressed. In *Shalom in the Community of Creation,* Cherokee theologian Randy Woodley argues that Native Americans are oriented by a worldview he calls the *harmony way,* where generosity and hospitality are integral to maintaining harmonious relations in community.

> Stinginess in any regard does not stand in Indian country. . . . The formal adoption process among Native Americans is an extension of a deep and profound sense of hospitality to others. Constant visiting among friends and relatives is a hallmark of Native American communities, and no one ever goes away from a gathering hungry.

Complete strangers are often given special honor and gifts at pow-wows and at other social functions.[13]

We need to exercise prudence and judgment when risking hospitality, of course, but when we cease to open the door to the mystery of what's beyond—when we seek to become totally safe on our own terms—then we miss out on the dynamic movement of the Spirit.

• • •

Through prayer, fasting, confession and repentance, music, moral dialogue, the Circle of Care and other acts of hospitality, congregations have a unique role to play in the struggle for justice. When people draw energy from their congregational identity and the resources of their tradition, their engagement in broad-based initiatives is enhanced. And as we'll see, clergy and other faith leaders in particular can enhance the work of justice in broad-based initiatives by leaning into their traditions and leveraging the tools and training of their vocation.

• • •

Dear Alina and Yehsong:

While we need to engage in political and economic advocacy, faith communities should not just join in the strategies practiced by the overall coalition. Be both humble and bold; respect the leadership of the sectors that represent the organized poor, but recognize that we also, as people of faith, have unique strategies to contribute. Call on congregations to do what they can do best—the nurture of organizers and holistic organizing—and encourage them to bring all of their spiritual gifts and practices to the broader movement for justice.

Individual Gifts

Chaplaincy to the Poor and the Powerful

In 2010 the director of clergy organizing for the PICO National Network, Rev. Michael-Ray Matthews, started the "Prophetic Voices Initiative," a network of clergy who speak publicly for justice. This is a natural contribution for clergy to make: because much of their ministry involves communication, they are generally good at it, and in their congregations they have a ready audience to interact with what they have to say. But public speaking is not the only contribution faith leaders can make. Other powerfully useful gifts and skills can serve the broader movement.

Just one example is their capacity to act as chaplains on the field of the battle for justice. In military contexts, chaplains have made an important contribution by reminding soldiers of their deepest values and commitments, of who they love and what they believe, of what they are fighting for. Chaplains "en-courage" soldiers, enabling them to overcome fear and immediate self-interest to do what is right. Similarly, faith leaders have two important chaplaincy roles in the movement for justice—one with the powerful and one with the poor.

Moral Authority and Chaplaincy to the Powerful

In the typical advocacy process a group, with specific interests and an agenda to match, influences (or pressures) a policymaker to support the policies that meet their needs. In corporate campaigns, workers or customers similarly try to move the company to respond to their concerns and needs.

The word typically used in Alinsky-style organizing to describe the person in the position of power is *target*. In traditional advocacy, all of the strategic activities of the group are directed at the target. The question for the target is simple: will he or she gain more by doing what the group wants, denying what it wants, or compromising?

Faith traditions know that the choice of words is significant on multiple levels. The apostle James, for example, talks about the power of the tongue to create or destroy (James 3:3-12). So the broad use of the word *target* in organizing is troubling to faith-rooted organizing. The word has significant associations, many of them violent. What do we normally do with a "target"? What does it feel like to be on the other end of someone who views you as a target? Does it make you feel like meeting them halfway?

Policymakers and other people with power are more than targets; they are human beings. The Holy Spirit is always at work in the soul of every human being, pushing, prodding, provoking them to do God's will. We can be the ally of the Holy Spirit, supporting that part of a person that longs to respond.

Frederick Douglass, the great nineteenth-century civil rights leader, noted that power never concedes power without a demand. What he did not acknowledge is that the demand that moves the powerful person may arise not only from outside interests but also from the depths of his or her soul. The interaction between Pontius Pilate and Jesus (John 18:28-38) describes a powerful emotional moment when Pilate is clearly struggling with his soul. In the end, he chooses safety over truth, a choice often made in halls of power. However, it is not the only possible choice.

Another story about speaking truth to power and moving the soul is told in 2 Samuel 12. King David has had an affair with his neighbor's wife Bathsheba which resulted in pregnancy. Terrified of potential condemnation, David tries to manipulate events to cover up the pregnancy and ultimately has Bathsheba's husband set up to be killed in battle. David then marries Bathsheba and quietly takes her home to give birth to his son. The prophet Nathan, who has originally helped David to ascend to the throne, confronts him cleverly. "There were two men in a certain town, one rich and the other poor," he begins, asking for David's judgment in a case of exploitation. David calls for the death sentence for the offender, at which point Nathan—at the risk of his own life—accuses David of being the offender.

At that moment, a traditional organizing perspective would expect David to punish Nathan. Instead, David is personally convicted. He admits that Nathan is right and atones, seeking to re-establish justice and right relationship with God and his community.

While David's response is admittedly less common than Pilate's, it is always possible—even in the modern world. In 2004, 70,000 grocery workers in Southern California were out of work; 25,000 were on strike and another 45,000 were locked out. The most important issue for the striking workers was health insurance: the initial proposals from the company would push many workers toward already strained public health care systems. The company in charge of the leading grocery chain, a multi-industry corporation with a reputation for ruthless business dealings, had spent nearly forty-eight hours at a time at the negotiating table, and their proposals had barely moved. They did not seem to be seriously interested in negotiating. The strike began in October; by December, workers were losing their homes and cars, the health and welfare fund of the union was close to bankrupt, and workers were unable to obtain critically needed medicine and medical care.

The thought of tens of thousands of new clients depending on these fragile and threatened public health care systems was profoundly worrisome for many of the faith leaders in the region. But in December, CLUE staff received an unexpected report. The CEO of the multi-industry corporation had experienced a religious conversion. CLUE leaders pursued a moral dialogue with the CEO but were unable to obtain an opportunity to speak with him directly, so they decided to follow the example of the Old Testament prophets and carry out a public and symbolic action that might allow for an alternative form of communication.

CLUE planned a pilgrimage of prayer from Southern California to the grassy area outside the gate of the multi-million dollar housing development where the CEO lived. They brought with them 40,000 postcards and letters from the heads of every major religious denomination, asking him to return to the negotiating table, to stay until there was an agreement, and to compromise on health care. Having found out that he had just made a major philanthropic donation to stop puppy abuse, the clergy, congregation members, workers and workers' families who participated in the pilgrimage brought puppies with them. The pilgrimage was followed by Fox News; four journalists from different publications accompanied the marchers. At every stop along the way they held a prayer service and then spoke into the cameras, asking the CEO to look at the puppies, to raise his eyes to the children holding them, to further raise his eyes to their parents, and to ask himself what God would want him to do.

The CEO would not meet with the bishops who took the letters and postcards to the gate. He did, however, call his pastors, who met privately with a group of faith leaders who had participated in the pilgrimage—including a pastor who had been a leader in the civil rights movement. That group prayed together and entered into a deep discussion of scriptural imperatives with implications for the situation. Less than two weeks later, the CEO went back to the negotiating table, stayed for fourteen days and compromised. He also (quietly) put millions of his own money back into the health and welfare fund of the union to ensure that workers could obtain timely medical care. When the contract came back up for renewal three years later, there was no strike, and many of the medical benefits that had been lost were restored.

The CEO made a moral decision; he listened to the Holy Spirit and not merely to the call of money and power. This is significant: if a person in authority does what a group wants because of the pressure they apply, watch what happens if they turn their backs for a moment, need to focus elsewhere or lose intensity. If a leader undergoes a moral conversion or an awakening to the moral import of a decision, however, you don't need to continue to apply pressure in the same way. The pressure will now be internal and ongoing.

James Senegal, the CEO of Costco and a faithful Catholic, is known for business practices that are congruent with his faith. In 2002, sales in established Costco stores grew by 6 percent and exceeded those of its nearest competitor, the Walmart-owned Sam's Club. The figures were not good enough for many investors, however, who pointed out Costco's relatively low earnings on the dollar. According to critics, the problem was that Senegal was too generous to his employees. A cashier at Costco could earn up to $40,000 per year after four years of service, an unheard-of salary in the world of discount retail. Other retail-industry experts countered that Costco's generous compensation structure actually increased productivity and reduced loss due to turnover and theft. Senegal told the *Los Angeles Times,* "I don't see what's wrong with an employee earning enough to be able to buy a house or have a health plan for the family. We're trying to build a company that will be here 50 years from now."[1]

Another CEO, an active member of a CLUE congregation, shared that before he ran into CLUE, he had an invisible curtain down the middle of his being. On one side was the faithful member of his congregation. On the other side was a business leader, solely focused on increasing profit. When he heard faith leaders speaking about the call to moral choices in the context of a social contract mandated by God, however, the curtain came down and he had to face himself. It wasn't an easy experience, but he says the deeper sense of peace and inner integrity that he now has was worth the cost.

The work of the Holy Spirit extends beyond corporate leaders to public policymakers. They are more likely to make courageous moral choices, however, when the group meeting with them includes people who are also taking a risk, people who would have to make a sacrifice if the policy in question were to pass. When a group is making an argument based on self-interest, they may have a compelling argument, but they do not have moral authority. People whose demands involve their own sacrifice have moral authority; they themselves are making a difficult moral choice and therefore have the right to call others to the same choice.

Faith leaders in the Central American Sanctuary Movement of the 1980s, and many of the nonblack faith leaders involved with the American civil rights movement who were in solidarity with those most directly affected, had tremendous moral authority. Their core motivation was so clearly rooted in the common good that they were able to call policy-makers to a similar stand. Similarly, their *actions* were congruent with their message: they prioritized the perspective and message of the poor. They truly were in solidarity, amplifying the voices of those who were most directly affected even as they joined them.

To be a chaplain to powerful leaders is not merely to attempt to move or influence them but to *minister* to them. It is to call them to live up to their divine call, to draw from the centuries of spiritual resources of the church to enable them to overcome fear, greed and laziness to do what is right. It is to speak and manifest the truth. Like all chaplains, advocate chaplains pray fervently with and for those in their spiritual care as well as speaking the Word of God into their immediate situation. Advocate chaplains are not primarily concerned with passing a specific policy but rather with effec-tively calling the policymaker to create and champion policies that accom-plish God's will for the most vulnerable and promote the common good. This requires an ongoing relationship with the policymaker that is deep and value-based, not a brief visit when a policy campaign is "hot."

The congregations and denominations of which believing policy-makers are a part have a role to play in faith-rooted organizing as well. Pastors are often so paralyzed by the fear of controversy or the loss of income from major donors that they avoid controversial conversations with their congregants. When World Vision decided to take on AIDs in Africa, for example, the decision was enormously controversial; many pastors were reluctant to bring the project into their churches. One of the senior leadership responsible for managing the church campaign took an unusual approach to overcoming this fear; he asked the reluctant pastors if they were "ignorant" of the biblical requirement for the church to get involved, or if they were merely "disobedient." Surprisingly, the approach worked relatively well; it's possible that his courage in asking the question was in itself contagious.

An example from our Jewish brothers and sisters is worth considering. In 2005, CLUE LA leadership met with the leadership of the local rabbinical school to explore the creation of a course on economic justice. We came up with a strategy that we thought was very clever for ensuring that the course would have maximum current as well as future impact. We would invite major Jewish business leaders to participate in the course with the explicit goal of sharing their expertise on how young rabbis could most realistically and effectively talk about business ethics with their congregants. Of course, we hoped that the dialogue would impact the business owners themselves—particularly if we brought worker leaders and respected veteran rabbis into the room.

Much to our surprise, the business leaders who participated included some of the most prominent and highest level corporate founders and CEOs in the area, most of them in their seventies. They participated with an unexpected motive: they were concerned about their sons. Their rabbis had been influential in teaching them the social contract in a way that profoundly affected their business practices, but they feared that later generations had become soulless—only concerned about profit in a way that was detrimental for the whole society, including the business community. These older business professionals ended up challenging the young rabbinical students (who were anxious about losing their jobs if they confronted their wealthier members) to be tougher and to take more risks in advocacy.

Chaplaincy should not just work as an isolated set of relationships. It should always be in the context of "surround sound," an overall educational effort by the faith community to teach principles of justice that have real-life consequences. As an example, a broad coalition was working on statewide health-care policy in California, when a Republican legislator in the Central Valley heard a sermon by his bishop on health care; as part of the service he was given materials presenting the faith case for healthcare policy. That legislator walked into the office of the Republican governor, a fellow Catholic, with those materials and exhorted him to move on the issue.

A few years later a federal healthcare bill came up, and another devout Central Valley legislator was on the fence. On the morning of that vote, an op-ed piece by Catholic and Lutheran bishops showed up in his daily newspaper, and he received a call from a major evangelical leader. Although there was enormous opposition in his district, he voted his conscience and supported the bill. This legislator knew he would be attacked for his action, but he placed his accountability to the Holy Spirit higher than his responsibility to his donors. The bishops who wrote the op-ed piece and the evangelical leader who called him served as chaplains on the battlefield for God's justice, reminding him to live by his deepest beliefs and values regardless of the consequences.

Chaplains to the Poor

Jose was a hotel worker from El Salvador, the single father of six children. When he became involved in a campaign in his hotel to hold on to their family health insurance, he quickly became a leader. Around that time his best friend at work, a onetime worker of the year, was fired—apparently in retribution for her leadership in the struggle. Jose was frightened and went to his pastor for advice, fully expecting to be told to forget all of that union business and take care of his family.

Jose's pastor was an Irish immigrant to the United States, a cultural tradition which often supports the fight for justice. The pastor assured Jose that he should not be afraid: the God of the exodus was a God of justice. At that moment, Jose says, he felt a rush of power from his head to his feet, and he was no longer afraid. He knew he was fighting for his children and the other workers' children to be respected as children of God, as worthy of health care as wealthy children. He knew that this was a holy fight, and if he were to lose his job he would find another one. He knew that he wanted his children to see him live out of faith and not out of fear. He realized that if God was with him, who could be against him?

Fear is contagious; so is courage. When Jose returned to the struggle fearless and full of faith, he inspired his coworkers; in the power of their unity, they eventually won their battle.

CLUE leaders have been chaplains for many workers and other poor people who must take serious risks in their struggle for justice. This kind of chaplaincy is rooted in respect, the knowledge that poor and oppressed people are often more able to carry the cross and bear a serious sacrifice than those who are more financially and socially secure. Dolores Huerta tells a story about when she first came to work with Cesar Chavez. He gave her the task of collecting union dues—the only income for organizers. Chavez refused to raise funds from outside, a strategy that would have provided middle-class salaries for organizers. Instead, the organizers lived hand to mouth, at the same level of the farmworkers, and dependent on their support. Chavez saw this as essential to the empowerment of the workers and their ownership of the union. Union dues were $3.50 per month. In addition to supporting organizers, they also funded a small disability and death benefit for members. At the time, farmworkers were earning about $.70 an hour; $3.50 would buy a bag of potatoes, a dozen eggs, tortillas and a pound of beans, but workers chose to pay the dues.

Early in her relationship with the union Huerta approached a small chicken shack where a single mother lived. The mother was absent, but her teenage daughter was home. The daughter accused Huerta of taking the only money the family had to buy dinner. Huerta went back to Chavez and told him she could not continue to do this work. Chavez asked her if she thought she could bear the cross. When she responded that she could, he asked her why she thought this farmworker mother would be unable to bear the cross; in fact, he told her, this woman would be more able to bear the cross than Huerta would.

Huerta returned to the chicken shack. The woman was there and apologized for her daughter's rudeness, handing over the union dues. Later, after the campaign succeeded and the workers achieved living wages, the daughter approached Huerta, weeping, and thanked her for believing in them.

Chaplaincy to and with the poor and oppressed is characterized by truth-telling, by acting with integrity and by prayer. If they have prayerfully chosen to participate in civil disobedience, chaplains must be ready to accompany those they minister with to jail, as did the U.S. civil rights and sanctuary leaders. Inside the holding cell, chaplains can minister to their fellow detainees, leading them in prayer and speaking words of encouragement, offering testimony to all of the prisoners and the guards.

When I (Alexia) was arrested in a civil disobedience action many years ago, a young Korean policeman wearing a cross reacted with distress. He said to me, "Pastor, you are going to have a criminal record." I responded that Jesus also had a criminal record. I believe this simple interchange created an important moment of insight for that police officer that may have affected his future thinking and behavior in multiple ways.

When advocate chaplains accompany and suffer with the victims of injustice, they have the capacity to reframe the way the victims are portrayed by the larger society. They make them visible as God sees them. In December 2005, the Sensenbrenner Bill passed the House of Congress, making it a felony to be an undocumented immigrant, or to help or serve an undocumented immigrant. Anti-immigrant sentiment was running high; immigrants were being portrayed publicly as invaders, drains on the economy and threats to national security. While the bill was still pending passage in the Senate, on Ash Wednesday of 2006 Cardinal Roger Mahoney of the Archdiocese of Los Angeles called upon Catholics across the country to continue to serve all people who came to them in need, regardless of their immigration status—even if they were to go to jail for it. His sermon made undocumented immigrants visible as human beings, brothers and sisters in God's family. It provoked a different tone in the congressional debate, thanks to the voice and role of faith leaders in the conversation. A new Sanctuary Movement gradually started up in 2006, with faith leaders across the country standing with immigrants and risking their own status.

A family had fled the Guatemalan civil war after the father of the family was assassinated. The mother and the smallest children received political asylum in the United States, but the eldest son, Juan, stayed for a few more years before finally barely escaping with his life. Because of the delay, however, his asylum petition was refused.

Juan appealed, and a court date was set with an immigration judge. Unfortunately, a letter changing the date of the hearing was delivered to the wrong address in his building, only getting to him after the hearing had passed. In his absence he was given a deportation order. His case could only be reopened by special action of the judge who had given the order, or by the field office director for Los Angeles. Neither of them was willing to review the case.

Rev. Cesar Arroyo, a Peruvian Lutheran pastor of a primarily undocumented congregation in the San Fernando Valley, decided to take Juan into sanctuary in his little church. Rev. Arroyo shared openly with Juan that this was risky for him in more than one way; he was petitioning for his son to immigrate legally to the United States at the time. (He was accurate about the risk; his son's paperwork was "lost" three times, causing a delay of several years.) Juan asked why Rev. Arroyo was willing to take such a risk; he replied, "It is the privilege of the cross."

The power of this pastor's faith ended up inspiring courage and faith not only in Juan but in a much larger circle of people. When the anti-immigrant protest group the Minutemen started planning a weeks-long action of heckling and threatening church members during their worship services, the pastor let his congregation know they were not expected to come. The first Sunday of the Minutemen's planned action, however, members of other sanctuary churches and the Lutheran bishop attended the worship service in solidarity. There almost wasn't room for them; the congregation followed their pastor's example of courage and faith and attended services as usual. After church, the congregation members, along with the visiting sanctuary church members and the bishop, walked in a procession around the church, singing, and then stopped in front of the Minutemen to pray for them. After the prayer, the pastor returned to the church building and said, "God Bless America!" Not quite knowing what to do, the Minutemen replied "God Bless America!" They never returned to heckle at that church again. A hard-bitten Univision reporter had never seen anything like this; he told the congregation, "You all might even make me into a Christian!"

The Poor and Powerful Together

At times chaplaincy to the oppressed and to powerful leaders intersects in creative and powerful ways. "Juan," a big, burly immigrant from central Mexico, had been a boxer but became a chef in a luxury hotel which for over twenty-five years had benefited from union representation. Because of union standards for wages and health benefits, Juan was able to buy a modest home and send his children to college. In 2000, however, his hotel was sold to a new owner and closed for months of renovation. The whole workforce was laid off, and when the hotel reopened, none of the former workers was rehired. Needless to say, the hotel reopened without union representation and offered very low wages to its new workforce. Juan was called on to help to fight to bring back the original workers and restore their living wages and benefits. He hesitated, feeling like he lacked the formal education and confidence to fight in this very different arena.

Juan's pastor, the leader of one of the largest Catholic churches in the country, was not a big fan of unions in general and of the hotel union in particular. However, when Juan came with downcast eyes and asked for his help, he couldn't refuse. His initial response was fairly minimal. He promised that the Monday mass would include prayers for the workers and their families.

Many workers attended that Monday mass; their tears and stories began to affect the pastor. Juan asked him to meet with a group of workers and pray for them, and by the end of the prayer meeting, the pastor agreed to attend a city council hearing on the issue.

Juan testified at the city council meeting, sharing a story about his disabled daughter. "When my daughter was diagnosed with a heart problem that would require an expensive operation, the doctors told us that they could not save her. I went home and cried, because I am only a poor Mexican immigrant with little education, but then I realized that my daughter was not only the child of a poor immigrant. She was also a child of God; her life deserved to be saved just as much as any other child of God. So I went back to the doctors and I fought for her to have the operation. And I won! My daughter is alive today, and she is a blessing to everyone who knows her.

"I have realized," Juan continued, "that this fight for our hotel is the same kind of fight. We are children of God; we deserve living wages and health benefits for our hard work. I am here before you, even though I may not be much in your eyes, because I know how God sees us all—the value that we all have in God's eyes."

The pastor, with tears streaming down his face, stood to testify. He began by telling the council that he had just learned the meaning of faith, after over twenty-five years in the priesthood. He then argued for a worker retention policy that would hold the new owner accountable to give preference to workers with many years of excellent service to the hotel. The struggle went on for years, but Juan and his pastor stayed with it until the workers won. The hotel became known again for its good treatment of its workforce and the quality of the service it provided to its guests.

In this instance Juan and his pastor acted as chaplains for each other, inspiring each other on the field of the battle for justice. The poor can also act as chaplains for each other. When the labor organization Change to Win began to organize an association of warehouse workers in the Inland Empire in southern California, they faced a near-impossible challenge. The Inland Empire is a severely economically depressed area (the second highest percentage of foreclosures in the country). Inland Empire workers depend desperately on their jobs, which pay minimum wage and offer no benefits. Most of them are vulnerable—immigrants, ex-offenders, high-school dropouts—and are employed through temporary agencies. Many of the warehouses flout basic labor rights with impunity. Working conditions resemble factories in the Global South, with no ventilation in 108-degree weather, flimsy gloves that fall apart and allow solvent to burn holes into workers' hands, or unsanitary conditions in which, for example, workers catch fungi from cleaning out used tennis shoes for resale overseas. When one "temporary" worker in a Walmart-controlled warehouse submitted an OSHA complaint, no one on his shift was invited back.

When a new secretary of labor indicated that she would be willing to prosecute the warehouses as well as the temporary agencies, Warehouse Workers United was excited, but they knew they had to help the workers overcome their fears enough to testify. CLUE in the Inland Empire developed a program, led by an organizer who had been trained in the El Salvador movement, to help warehouse workers become "chaplains on the field of battle" for their coworkers. An initial sixteen-week training program turned into a weekly meeting of a cohort of fearless and inspirational leaders. A year after the program started, sixty workers testified about workplace abuses. The program has since given birth to a national Walmart worker peer chaplaincy, in which Walmart retail workers of faith are trained to inspire and sustain their coworkers as they struggle for respect and living wages with the largest company in the world.

Faith-rooted organizing calls and equips people of faith to be chaplains to the powerful and the poor alike, a unique gift with powerful impact on the broader movement for social and economic justice. However, we must always be aware of the complexities inherent in embodying the role of chaplain.

Lovers in a Dangerous Time

Swiss theologian Karl Barth had a strong aversion to the idea of military chaplains. In his *Epistle to the Romans* he writes,

> Fulfill your duties without illusion, but no compromising of God! Payment of tax, but no incense to Caesar! Citizens initiatives and obedience but no combination of throne and altar, no Christian Patriotism, no democratic crusading. Strike and general strike, and streetfighting if needs be, but *no* religious justification and glorification of it! Military service as soldier or officer if needs be but under *no* circumstances army chaplain! Socialdemocratic but *not* religious socialist! The betrayal of the gospel is *not* part of your political duty![2]

Barth had long observed a dangerous tendency within the German church that led to it being domesticated by the nation-state, betraying the heart of the gospel. While Hitler claimed to be the *Führer*, lord and healer of Germany, Christianity believes that Jesus Christ is the Lord and Healer of the world. Hitler and the Nazis made a category mistake by trying to take authority that is given only to God, who is revealed in Jesus Christ.

Barth first renounced the liberal theological tradition in which he had been trained when he saw it capitulating to the Kaiser in World War I. "An entire world of theological exegesis, ethics, dogmatics, and preaching, which up to that point I had accepted as basically credible, was thereby shaken to the foundations, and with it everything which flowed at that time from the pens of the German theologians."[3] Barth saw that his professors had been quickly colonized by the power of Prussian militarism, powers that did not embody the radical social ethic of the gospel. He repudiated the "*Kultur Protestantismus*" which provided a theological justification for a bourgeois acceptance of worldly ideologies like Nazism.

While Barth was skeptical of military chaplains, his critique really raises the question of how, in an age of war, we can be lovers of Christ and neighbor. How can we have the strength to love our enemies? This takes a special courage. Releasing this courage is the call of the faith-rooted chaplain.

Established by the Episcopal Church in 1834, the Seaman's Church Institute promotes the safety, dignity and improved working environment for the men and women serving in North American and international maritime workplaces. I (Peter) worked for the Seaman's Church Institute as an industrial chaplain for New York and New Jersey, ministering to seafarers on container ships out of Port Newark. When I would board the ships, the Filipino seafarers would often give me a handful of one hundred dollar bills and tell me to wire it back to their wives and children in Manila. They asked me to pray for them, but I found that what they really wanted was for me to listen to them. After listening with my heart to the tales the seafarers shared with me, I would pray for them.

Dietrich Bonhoeffer writes,

> Many people are looking for an ear that will listen. The person who no longer listens to their brother or sister will soon no longer be listening to God. . . . One who cannot listen long and patiently will presently be talking beside the point and never really speaking to others, albeit they be not conscious of it.[4]

As chaplains we need to listen "long and patiently," discerning the heart and soul of what the person is saying. As we listen attentively, we can begin to discern what the Spirit is saying through them. Then we are able to respond by the Spirit in our questions and conversations, as well as through our prayers.

In addition to being attentive listeners, we also encourage those we are working with in the movement. Movement work is exhausting, so we need to encourage people to take heart. As encouragers, we actually help people claim the courage they have in their hearts. As Parker Palmer writes,

Two thousand years ago Rabbi Hillel asked three questions that remain worth asking: "If I am not for myself, who will be? If I am only for myself, what am I? And if not now, when?" For those of us who want to see democracy survive and thrive—and we are legion—the heart is where everything begins: that grounded place in each of us where we can overcome fear, rediscover that we are members of one another, and embrace the conflicts that threaten democracy as openings to new life for us and for our nation.[5]

When our hearts are courageous to fight for justice and strengthened to love, we can be more gracious and fruitful movement builders. When we incarnate spiritual presence, we don't need to preach it; people can see it and smell it. "A rose does not need to preach," Mahatma Gandhi wrote. "It simply spreads its fragrance. The fragrance is its own sermon . . . much finer and subtler than that of the rose." Having such a fine and subtle spirituality, however, requires a lifetime of spiritual discipline. As Stephen Kim Sou-hwan, the late senior cardinal in Korea, has said, "Love through head and mouth does not carry fragrance. Understanding, generosity, acceptance, assimilation, and humility are proceeded in real love. It took me 70 years for love to come down from my head to my heart." A faith-rooted organizer is committed to exercising their heart in practicing the spiritual disciplines, in order to be able to fully love.

Martin Buber in his book *I and Thou* talks about two types of ways we can relate to people—the instrumental way (I-It) or the personal way (I-Thou). In faith-rooted organizing we are not interested merely in what someone can do for us; we are genuinely interested in people as children of God. Once we recognize the dignity of the other, however, how do we relate to them? In his lectures on psychotherapy, Buber suggests that while we may associate the exchange of hearts with the erotic intimacy of lovers, we in fact exchange our hearts with close friends and sometimes even with strangers.[6] As humans we know how to love because we were created by a God who is love (1 John 4:8). Buber describes God as the Thou who "whatever else he may be . . . enters into a direct relation with us men in creative, revealing and redeeming acts, and thus makes it possible for us to enter into a direct relation with him."[7] God is a living, active, personal, vital, communal, transcendent being whom we revere and worship as a Thou. And when we are spiritually aligned with God as a Thou, we are better able to treat other human beings as thous, offering them the tender love and deep respect that they deserve as fellow humans created and loved by God.

Chaplains bridge the gap between the love of God as a Thou and the acknowledgment of the thou-ness of the poor and powerful alike. In faith-rooted organizing our opponents are not targets but fellow human beings, made in the image of God, acted on by the Spirit of a loving God, called to do their part in the battle for justice and human dignity.

• • •

Dear Alina and Yehsong:

Warriors on the battlefield for justice need chaplains to remind them of what they believe and who they love so that they are not disabled by fear and loss. The powerful and the poor, the privileged and the oppressed, all alike need moral en-couragement. If the faith community doesn't bring this gift, no one will.

8

Prophetic Advocacy and Public Witness

The special gifts that believers bring to broader movements for justice can be categorized in language which echoes the early church's description of the mission of Jesus. As disciples of Jesus the prophet, priest and king, we are called to continue his priestly work (manifested in prayer and chaplaincy) but also the prophetic aspects of his ministry.

The prophet speaks the word and calling of God into a historic context. He or she addresses root causes of social problems—including the flawed structures and systems created by and reinforcing human sin. The prophet exposes the lies societies believe that legitimize injustice, and convey the sacred truths that counteract those lies. Prophets reveal the ways that societies institutionalize sin and the sweeping changes necessary to cleanse and heal our institutions, so that people are free to become all God intended them to be. Prophets cast the vision for a healthy society with just structures that ensure fair treatment for all and support the fullness of life for every child.

Faith-rooted organizing enables us to go beyond developing small examples of healthy community to address, in the manner of the prophets, the brokenness of the broader society.

The Prophetic Power of Symbols

A great choreographer once said that if you can explain a dance, it is not a very good dance. We have a treasure trove in the faith community of symbols, rituals and music that can multiply the impact of our messages if we choose to utilize them in our public communication.

In Jeremiah 19, God instructs the prophet Jeremiah to break a potter's earthenware jug on the ground in front of the elders of the people. In John 13, Jesus washes the feet of his disciples. In all three Synoptic Gospels, Jesus breaks the bread and blesses the wine of his last supper before he is taken away to be killed. All of these actions were ways that God communicated prophetic messages—more powerful than words alone could ever be.

In traditional advocacy, policy wonks assume that the general populous makes decisions on the basis of logic and self-interest; if they receive facts tied to clear arguments about the policies that will benefit them, they will support those policies. There is ongoing evidence, however, that the policy experts are by and large mistaken. The average person makes decisions on the basis of a complex set of factors which include emotion and relationship as well as logic and facts. Truth can be accessed in different ways through all of these avenues, and all of the great faith traditions speak to both the left-brained values of logic and facts, and the right-brained values of emotion and relationship.

When the CLUE affiliate in San Diego (the Interfaith Committee for Worker Justice) prayed before the city council for the poor of the city, the well-being of the city and the courage and wisdom of the council, their advocacy went beyond logical argument. A conservative member of the council was moved by these prayers to vote for living wage legislation; the prayer had communicated to his heart and soul in a way that all of the logical talking points in the world could not.

In front of a major business in another California city, corporate managers saw workers with multiple injuries from their mandated acceleration of production take part in a healing service; some of those managers were provoked to re-evaluate the human impact of their workplace procedures.

In 2006, the majority of Los Angeles security officers earned very low wages and were given no benefits for their dangerous work. The building owners used a bidding process that rewarded the lowest bid from a number of small guard companies. CLUE worked in partnership with the Service Employees International Union (SEIU) to convince the Building Owners and Managers' Association to pass a policy encouraging its members to do responsible contractor bidding, placing a floor on bids so that guard companies could pay living wages and provide health benefits. A key turning point in this campaign came when a group of African American pastors and congregants held a gospel prayer service in the lobby of the headquarters of one of the largest building owners. The police came to stop the service but were not able to figure out who was in charge. When they talked to a pastor about stopping, an elderly sister began to wail and pray in the Spirit; when they approached her, an eleven-year-old began to sing. Gradually a number of building tenants joined in the prayer service, and ultimately the owners invited the faith leaders and workers up for a conversation.

In 1998, some hotel owners were negotiating a contract in good faith, but others were trying instead to break the union of hotel workers. CLUE volunteer leader Rabbi Neil Comess-Daniels of Santa Monica proposed a symbolic act: during Holy Week and right before Passover, over a hundred faith leaders led a procession down Rodeo Drive in Beverly Hills, bringing milk and honey to the owner who was negotiating in good faith, and delivering bitter herbs to the others. One of the hotel owners, a person of faith, had never before seen his management decisions as a moral issue, and within several weeks he began to negotiate in good faith. The idea has since been replicated across the country.

At another point in a long low-wage workers' struggle with multinational corporations, we handed out small stones to striking workers with the words "Strength and Support" in multiple languages. We reminded the workers of the story of David and Goliath, in which five small stones had been more powerful than a mighty giant.

In Santa Monica in 2002, a coalition of labor, community and faith leaders learned that a number of luxury hotels had benefitted from $180 million in public subsidies from the city while paying their workers so little that they were eligible for public benefits. The hotel owners were

essentially double-dipping in the public trough. The coalition proposed
legislation that would require companies with over $5 million in income
per year to pay a wage high enough to make a family of four ineligible for
food stamps. The luxury hotels hired a consultant whose website proclaimed that he could defeat any initiative for $1 million. The plan in-
volved spending over $2 million to develop and promote an alternative
"living wage" bill that would restrict the living wage to city workers. Day
laborers dressed in rented hotel worker uniforms and stood on street
corners with signs supporting the false living wage bill; the hotels also
paid people to go door to door with misleading flyers. Faith leaders involved in the coalition decided that a prophetic and symbolic response
was required, so we created a six-foot-high cardboard cutout of a biblical
prophet and made a banner saying "Prophets in the Marketplace." We
then stood on the Promenade (a popular outdoor local mall) in an arc,
alternating clergy and hotel workers. The clergy read from the biblical
prophets about the danger of corrupt leaders while hotel workers shared
about their daily struggles with poverty. Meanwhile, students handed out
flyers debunking the false living wage bill. We repeated the action at the
Farmer's Market, adding a pie chart that showed the workers' compensation in comparison to the income of the hotels and the salaries of the
management, and then handing out free tiny pieces of pie—the approx-
imate size of the workers' share of the hotels' prophets. The false living
wage bill failed—80 percent to 20 percent.

Symbolism doesn't just move the observers of an action; it can encourage the participants in the action as well. On Century Boulevard near
the LAX airport, three hundred people were arrested in a sit-in. Many of
the arrestees were immigrants who were understandably frightened. The
organizers of the action wanted to give the participants some symbol of
support to give them peace and strength in their moment of trial, but arrestees are stripped of all belongings. They finally decided on a ritual of
breaking bread. Each person got a small piece. The symbolism stopped
short of a liturgy of holy Communion, given the religious diversity of the
participants, but the symbol still had immense power, reminding participants that they were not alone and that no one could take away God's

nurturing love from them no matter where they were.

Symbolic communication can happen on many levels of the organizing process—not just in the moments of public encounter. I will never forget the hotel housekeeper who stood before a congregation to share her suffering, struggle and hope. As she gazed at the faces of the brothers and sisters whose understanding and support she needed, all she could do was cry. The reaction of the congregation was remarkable; for the first time, many members made a real commitment to getting involved in justice ministries. Symbols can also function as "demonstration plots" that can later be brought to bear on larger movements. Cesar Chavez tended an organic garden as a reminder of God's providence, a call to healthy living and a sign that the toxic chemicals used in agribusiness that were harming farmworkers were not necessary.

Prayerfully offering spiritual gifts is an important faith-rooted organizing strategy because it taps into the prophetic imagination and sensitive conscience within each one of us. In the New York City Living Wage Movement, instead of using instrumental tactics and power politics to persuade public servants to pass the bill, we used symbols of faith to inspire them. When we visited with Speaker Christine Quinn's staff in December 2011, Rabbi Michael Feinberg presented a menorah and spoke about the meaning of the light of hope. We gave Quinn a framed photograph of Mother Teresa and, because Quinn is Irish Catholic, appealed to Catholic social thought by referring to Monsignor John Augustine Ryan's classic *A Living Wage*.[1] Imam Al-Hajj Talib 'Abdur-Rashid closed the meeting out with a brief Muslim devotion and prayer to Allah. That day we stood boldly as an interfaith coalition for economic justice, bringing the most beautiful treasures from our traditions with prayerful anticipation that our public servants would respond. A month later, a deal was negotiated to take the Living Wage Bill to a vote in the city council.

The Art of Organizing

Being a good faith-rooted organizer entails being an artist and improviser. Creativity is critical to reaching the hearts and souls of those we are inviting to join the struggle for justice. Current brain research is helping us better understand the creative process and the power of religious symbols and experiences. In fact, our brain can actually serve as a model for the communities we want to attain if we take seriously the latest neurology.

Our brains are incredibly complex embodiments of what scientists call emergent complexity. Essentially, this means that the sum is greater than the individual parts. The left side of the brain is traditionally linked to logic and facts, the right side of the brain correspondingly to emotion, intuition and images. It is vital, however, that we tap into the left side as well as the right side. Together they help us discern all that can be known about the objects of our inquiry.

Catherine Malabou's book *What Should We Do with Our Brain?* discusses the brain's ability to give form, receive form and destroy form.[2] Malabou's concept of neural plasticity means that the brain possesses a form of freedom. The brain is not hierarchical; it is the site of the interplay of creative forces of reception, formation and destruction. Malabou concludes the book with a picture of the brain and the world that is dynamic, not static; creative, not repetitive. This is good news for organizers, as we seek to move the world in some manner from where it is to a better, more just place to inhabit.

It should not surprise us that the nonhierarchical model of faith-rooted organizing is compatible with the biochemistry of the brain. Rather than simply acquiescing to a particular environment as we find it, we begin our attempt to establish order in the world with awareness—of the other, of the reality of human dignity and those factors in a situation that inhibit it. This kind of active *adaptability* is comparable to the neural plasticity that allows our brain to engage meaningfully in our body's environment.

The social environment we find ourselves in today is increasingly shaped by consumer capitalism. We can acquiesce to this environment by becoming ravenous consumers, buying products to fill the holes within our soul and racking up credit card debt. But we also have the opportunity to actively resist this way of being in the world. As Clayton Crocket and Jeffrey Robbins write, "The brain is not simply a biological organ but the site and sign of creative transformation."[3] The reality of neural plasticity gives us the power to reject the powers of this world and instead aspire to communities of love and justice—a revolutionary, prophetic aspiration, considering our current context.

There is a fundamental, *biological* grounding to our desire to shape our surroundings and in turn to be shaped by them. Philosopher Hans-Georg Gadamer gets at this through his notion of "play." In his magisterial *Truth and Method*, Gadamer explains that a work of art—whether a piece of art, a jazz tune or a scriptural narrative—has its existence within the interactivity (or "play") of text and community. To interpret a text is to enter into this play. Gadamer writes, "All encounter with the language of art is an encounter with an unfinished event and is itself part of this event."[4] From composition to interpretation to performance, texts are in motion; they are an "unfinished event." We are affected by art, but we also affect the art.

We see this dynamic in the call and response form of African American preaching. The preacher calls, and the people respond: "Amen, brother! Amen, sister!" Then the people call and the preacher responds. Throughout the sermon they build a synergistic dynamism, ultimately bringing the community to a collective catharsis. Similarly, there is a creative dynamic, an improvisational dimension to our own development as humans, which extends to our faith-rooted organizing.

Improvisation is integral to jazz; it involves being open to playing old songs in new ways, and writing new music for a new day. While driven by spontaneity, freedom and innovation, however, improvisation is never so unstructured or so wholly new that it could be considered *creatio ex nihilo*, a creation out of nothing. Rather, it is a *creatio continua*, drawing on existing materials to make music in new ways. Improvisation is the creative deployment of traditions and forms that are *at hand*, a constant negotiation of constraint and possibility. God the Creator created us to improvise.[5]

The faith-rooted imagination is ignited and sustained by the symbolic power of things *at hand*. The words of Holy Scripture provide the faith-rooted organizer with many different modes of artistic discourse, including narratives, prophecies, poems, proverbs, wisdom sayings, hymns, prayers and liturgies. These different genres access different dimensions of our souls and the souls of those we seek to move to new action. Waking up to pray and read Scripture helps to regulate our emotions, warms up our brain processing and ignites our prophetic imagination, offering a vision that is different from the vision of consumer capitalism that dominates our world.

Going to church and participating in its liturgies awakens us to what I call *festival time,* giving us the imagination to transform places of despair into spaces of hope.[6] As William Cavanaugh writes, "Globalization . . . enacts a universal mapping of space typified by detachment from any particular localities. . . . This detachment from the particular is actually used as a discipline to reproduce divisions between rich and poor, and . . . it produces fragmented subjects."[7] Christian liturgy, by contrast, initiates us into *festival time,* a way to be in the world in contrast to the rituals of consumer capitalism. The poetic nature of liturgy awakens the authenticity of our feelings, making us better able to engage the suffering of our fellow humans and opens a pathway for our creative, revolutionary action.

Powerful examples of theo-dramatic enactment for justice have emerged in the South Bronx, New York. The South Bronx is the poorest congressional district in the country. However, as theologian Ray Rivera has argued, the fires of God's Spirit have been burning in the chests of a new generation of faith-rooted organizers, including Alexie Torres-Fleming, the Latina founder of Youth Ministries for Peace and Justice (YMPJ).[8]

YMPJ used religious symbols to unveil the injustices in the community and ignite the prophetic imagation of the people. At the end of the forty days of Lent, Torres-Fleming would lead a procession called the "Way of the Cross" through the neighborhood. Often called the *Via Dolorosa* ("the Way of Sorrows") and displayed in stations on interior church walls with icons or sculptures, the Way of the Cross is a series of artistic representations of Jesus Christ carrying the cross to his crucifixion. YMPJ sought to break through the wall between the Word and world, and took this holy procession to the streets of the Bronx to engage the powers and principalities of the world. During this procession young people carried small crosses as they visited various "stations" in the Bronx. At each station they "crucified" common injustices in the community by naming them and nailing them to a larger cross carried by Father Juan Carlos Ruiz.

For example, the Bronx River, which should have been a source of life and happiness for the community, had been neglected and used as a dump. YMPJ named it the sin of pollution and nailed their prophetic denunciation to Father Ruiz's cross. Full of old cars, tires and oil, the ritual by the riverside was a prayer for purification. The liturgy was cathartic for the community, tapping into people's hearts, transforming bad emotional memories into new and positive ones. As Torres-Fleming recalls, "When you walk into a Catholic Church you dip your hand in holy water as well as when you depart to remember the blessing of baptism. So for us the river represented coming and going into a sacred place. As people of faith, we saw the Bronx river as holy water."[9]

Through taking the liturgies of the church outside into the community, we disrupt the daily routine of the city, awakening people from their spiritual slumber and provoking their conscience to feel injustices once again. The apostle Paul poetically describes the longing of creation in his epistle to the Romans as "groaning as in the pains of childbirth" to be redeemed (Romans 8:22). There is a deep interconnectedness between the human community and the community of creation, and visiting the river on the Way of the Cross was an opportunity for the people of the South Bronx to worship the Creator and commit to the redemption of the community.[10]

At other stations throughout the Bronx, this parade of young people were reminded that just as Jesus was condemned to death, through gun violence and drug overdoses many young people in their community were being condemned to death. Thus, the youth nailed the word *violence* to the cross. The procession continued to the Sheridan Expressway, The Concrete Plant, the sewer system, James Monroe High School and the Bronx River Public Housing Project, to bring light on other injustices in the community. After visiting each station and physically nailing the particular sin of that station onto the cross, the young people would join together in singing a praise chorus in English and Spanish: "Jesus, remember me, when you come into your kingdom. . . . Jesús, recúerdanos cuando éntres en tu reino." Given all of the injustices of the South Bronx, Jesus became a living incarnate reality of a love stronger than death. As the season of Lent ends with Resurrection Sunday, so the YMPJ's procession ended with the resurrection: the Way of the Cross liberated the people's imagination regarding their prophetic, moral agency to fight for freedom in the South Bronx.

Liberation theologian John Sobrino talks about "the crucified people as the presence of Christ crucified in history."[11] YMPJ is effective because it dramatizes the plight of the people in the Bronx. By taking our liturgies to the streets, we can reimagine the space and time currently reigned over by consumerism, baptizing the community into festival time. From the ancient ringing words of Scripture to our symbols, ceremonies, music and rituals, we have creative instruments for the transformation of perspectives and the conversion of hearts that go far beyond analysis and policy recommendations. When we seek to spread new ideas among humanity, we can turn to story, poetry, music and movement to inspire the heart and imagination—in our private conversations with the powerful, in formal hearings before official bodies, and in the streets.

•   •   •

Dear Alina and Yehsong:

Movements for justice often depend on logical arguments to make their case. This isn't bad, but it isn't enough.

In our faith traditions, we have colorful and emotionally powerful images and ancient actions to contribute that speak to the left and right brain alike.

Get creative! Dig deep in the wells of faith for all the beauty and power that is waiting there.

9

Recruitment

God's Pitchfork

One of the most common (and often most frustrating) challenges organizers face is recruitment. You cannot bring people together to create change unless you can bring them together. You have to get them off the couch, away from their blinking screens and out the door.

There are multiple theories in the field of organizing about motivation. Given that society offers a multitude of distractions that keep us from thoughtful reflection on the causes of pain and its potential solutions, and given that public messages about systems and policies (often paid for by those who are invested in the status quo) can be confusing to the average person, how do we motivate people to participate in the process of community change? How do we sustain their motivation?

Beyond Self-Interest

In 1980 I (Alexia) was taught by a traditional, Alinsky-based organizing network that effective motivation is always based in self-interest. The organizer learns to agitate community members so they awaken to the truth about the pain they feel and its systemic causes. The goal is for them to feel the anger that comes naturally from having one's self-interest thwarted by others. If we could get people to become angry enough at their public representatives, we could get them to storm down to City Hall and force officials to respond to the flaws in the system.

Anger is, physiologically, a force for change. Moreover, rage is a part of the prophetic experience. Prophets awaken people from their numbness to human suffering, and often the most immediate, natural and authentic human response to unjust suffering is anger. Of course, the continual nurturing of anger has a downside. *Chronic* anger is not physically healthy; it affects our blood pressure and other aspects of our biological systems in negative ways. The continual emphasis on anger also tends to create a culture in which confrontation seeps into all relationships, adding unnecessary stress and draining energy.

In 1984 I first visited the Philippines and encountered their movement for justice. An indigenous theology of suffering played a key role in their movement, and the faith sector was a respected contributor to the work of a broader coalition. I lived and ministered in the Philippines off and on from 1984 to 1987. One day I was trying to agitate a group of mothers around their self-interest so that they would come out for an upcoming march. They laughed at me. I asked why, and they responded that they thought my language and concepts were silly. The army was likely to shoot at the marchers; joining the march could mean death.

In that context, self-interest was not a motivation for participating in the march. So I asked them what would inspire or motivate them. They said they might come out to the march because of their love for their children.

I didn't understand; if they love their children, wouldn't they just get their children out of danger by migrating to another place?

Again they chided me gently. Our mutual faith, they reminded me, teaches us that all children are our children. A number of them ultimately joined the march; their faith and love motivated them to risk their very lives for the chance of creating a better world for all children.

Teresa Delgado, a Latina Catholic theologian, talks about the catalyst of faith which moves us into connection with a broader community and into the discovery of a collective sense of responsibility. Delgado's students document themselves on film trying to live on the salary of a Nike worker;

in their experiments they discover entirely different ways of understanding death and life, of deciding which kind of death they would be willing to live with. The church is continually being called, Delgado says, to be itself. In the community of the church we come to a personal, emotional understanding that those who seek to gain their individual lives will lose them, and those who lose their lives for the sake of the gospel will find them. Organizer Marshall Ganz talks about religion's capacity to inspire hope over fear, empathy over alienation and a sense of belovedness over worthlessness. As theologian Randy Woodley says, "I could be more human if I care for others at least as much as I care for myself."[1] Charlie Sherrod says it perhaps even more clearly: "Ain't nobody self-made. We all stand on the shoulders of our mama or daddy, our sisters, our brothers, our aunties or uncles, our great grandmas. We stand on their shoulders. And every time you admit that you get a little stronger."[2]

The Divine Pitchfork

Motivation, particularly for believers, is complex. The Holy Spirit moves in our hearts and lives in multiple and varied ways. The Greek word for *Spirit* in the New Testament, *paraclete,* is related linguistically to the word for "pitchfork." Many believers throughout history can relate to the experience of the great pitchfork, making us restless until we answer the call. Our souls are disturbed by the movement of God's Spirit and we will not be at peace until we respond.

That divine disturbance often comes from the Word of God. The cry embedded in it is God's desire for us to be compassionate, to awaken to the cries of the oppressed and the cries within our own soul.

I (Peter) learned about the importance of "the cry of Scripture" when I began participating in "scriptural reasoning," a movement that gathers Jews, Christians and Muslims to study their Scriptures together. Two of the founders of scriptural reasoning—David F. Ford, a Christian theologian at Cambridge University, and Peter Ochs, a Jewish theologian at University of Virginia—argue that the existential longing for liberation is at the heart of our Scriptures: as humans we are wounded, and the texts we compose bear those wounds; these same texts then motivate us to work for justice.

The words of Holy Scripture sensitize us as they humanize us.

In the book of Exodus, when the people of Israel are suffering in slavery, they cry out to God, and God responds: "The LORD said, 'I have indeed seen the misery of my people in Egypt. I have heard them crying out because of their slave drivers, and I am concerned about their suffering. So I have come down to rescue them from the hand of the Egyptians'" (Exodus 3:7-8). Aryeh Cohen suggests that in this passage "God articulates the explicit causality between being attentive to—*hearing*—the cries of the oppressed, and doing something about it—acting on it."[3] In contrast to Pharaoh, who hardens his heart and closes his ear to the suffering of the people, God hears the cry of the poor and responds through divine rescue. It is this activist, compassionate response to the cry of the poor that faith-rooted organizing seeks to emulate.

To be good readers of Scripture means to open our ears to the cry of the poor in the text of Scripture itself. I first encountered Scripture as a "wounded text" when I viewed Anselm Kiefer's painting *The Word* in the Tate Museum, on a cold day in London in December 1993. The large canvas, hung on a white wall by itself, was about twelve feet long. It was thick with black paint, scattered gray and brown, and little specks of red. In the middle of the painting was a physical bound book with brownish-white pages visible—aged, but resilient. I stood there for what seemed like an hour communing with the painting. In this dark warscape, full of suffering, sorrow and death, the Book—the Scripture of old—stood strong. Yet the Scripture was itself scattered and tattered, crying out in that painting in concert with the cries of those who were lost and those left behind grieving their loss. Standing before that painting, I was silenced.

As I looked at that painting I was reminded of the *Shoah*, in which six million Jews lost their lives through a systemic state-sponsored genocide in Nazi Germany. Why did they die? How did German society get to the place where they could allow such an atrocity? Why did other governments (including my own American government) remain silent for so long amidst the genocide? Why did God remain silent? These were the questions I pondered and continue to seek answers to through my prophetic activism.

Being a good scriptural reasoner means being open to hearing and responding to such cries of pain and suffering. To listen to the cry of the poor is not enough, we need to do something to help them and end the structures of greed in our society that are causing poverty. As Peter Ochs writes, "We who are in ear-shot of the cry are obligated to hear it and join in the work of healing."[4]

Over the years of faith-rooted organizing we have observed a number of ways in which God disturbs and animates us to action. The process and sources of motivation are remarkably individual. Just as Jesus never issued a general call for volunteers but rather called people by name, God calls us into a community of resistance and creation through the individual circumstances of our lives and our faith journeys. The more we understand this complex tapestry of motivation in each person, the more accurately we can fan the flames of inspiration in the people in our congregations and communities.

The Range of Spiritual Motivators

Compassion. Love can be the most powerful force on earth. One of World Vision's favorite prayers is "Let my heart break for that which breaks the heart of God." We all feel compassion at some point; many of us are moved by such compassion into action.

I (Alexia) was trained by my denomination to be a "mission developer" (church planter). As part of our training we were asked for our "banner scripture," the biblical passage that best describes our personal sense of calling. Mine was Matthew 9:35-36, in which Jesus looks at the crowds and has compassion for them. Having been raised outside of any religious tradition, part of what attracted me to the gospel was the compassion of Christ.

Compassion is an English word consisting of two Latin words—*com* meaning "with" and *passio* meaning "feel." In Matthew 9:35-36 Jesus looks at the crowds and *feels with* them—their pain as his pain, their hopes and dreams as his hopes and dreams. On a human level (beyond his divine mandate) his compassion compelled him to give his life for them. But in order for a person to feel that kind of compassion, he or she must first look into the hearts of the crowds and see what was hurting them and what they hoped for.

Jesus saw not only individuals but "the crowds." We see the problem and solution differently when we see and have compassion for the crowds. If you see one child struggling in school, for example, and you feel compassion for him, you tutor him. If you see a hundred children struggling in school, however, compassion for them compels you to work for the improvement of the school system. Jesus' compassion led him, for love's sake, to give all he had not just to isolated individuals but to the crowds—and ultimately to the world.

Different individuals are moved to compassion in different contexts. Rev. John Fife, one of the founders of the Central American Sanctuary Movement of the 1980s, speaks eloquently about an early experience of transporting refugees:

> I brought them to our house in Tucson. And just to see them safe for the first time since they'd left El Salvador and made the perilous journey through Guatemala, across Mexico and all those points, where their lives were hanging in the balance—literally. And then to say, okay, now you're home and you're going to be okay. And to watch that father and mother, watch them watch their kids and know that we made it. That kind of personal moment and realization is what committed us for the rest of the duration of time.[5]

I (Alexia) also had the experience of transporting a Sanctuary family to safety in the dead of night. The littlest baby was in a car seat, sleeping in front of me. All I could think of was my daughter as a baby and what it would have felt like to be separated from my child at that age.

When my daughter was thirteen, she volunteered for a summer for a community organizing campaign. They asked her to write the story of the events in her life that motivated her to join the campaign. Although she has directly and personally experienced racism and other forms of injustice, she chose instead to write about the hotel housekeepers and their children whom she had come to love growing up in the struggle. Her supervisor, an advocate of the Alinsky model of organizing, told her that this motivation was not valid; he asked her to rewrite the document to talk about those experiences that made her angry. He had failed to understand the power of compassion in her life; he had missed how compassion had compelled her to action in the movement for justice.

Sometimes compassion comes not from the experience of individual suffering but rather the suffering of a whole community or a whole society. On September 11, 2001, I (Peter) was supposed to be working for Fidelity Investments in the World Financial Center in New York City. When the World Trade Center Towers fell, they hit the World Financial Center. My job was lost; my life was saved. The next Sunday my wife, Sarah, and I went to Riverside Church to attend the morning worship service. Broken and unemployed, I longed in my spirit to serve in this moment of national crisis. Rev. Dr. James Forbes asked if there were any who wanted to volunteer at Ground Zero. I heard Christ calling in that moment and signed up after church, grateful for the opportunity to serve.

It was a cold, dark morning when we gathered at the church to ride the subway down to the still-smoldering Ground Zero. Among the acrid smoke and the dust of the souls lost that fateful day, I entered the closest thing to hell I have experienced in my life. I was asked to carry some crates of food to a food distribution center on the other side of Ground Zero, so I squinted through the air, opaque with ash, and walked through the long shadows of darkness cast from piles of debris and wreckage. A police officer who had fought in the Korean War told me he had never seen a war zone as bad as this. United in despair and brokenness, rescue workers, policemen, firemen, Red Cross workers, ministers and a host of volunteers entered a collective dark night of the soul. It was there that I felt the call to work for a new future, a more just city and a more peaceful world.

Gratitude. Compassion is only one of the deep spiritual sources of the motivation to do justice. Rabbi Leonard Beerman talks about the beginning of his lifelong commitment to justice being the "awareness that my life came up from some other place."[6] He says that to be grateful is to be aware of the connections that make your life possible.

Unitarian minister Sharon Welch works with a program in which middle- and upper-class students are introduced to organizing and advocacy. She asserts the effectiveness of beginning the process by awakening them to gratitude. Based on a recognition of their lifelong participation in a web of interconnection that sustains us all, she teaches them through experience and reflection that working for justice is a gift and blessing; it is a way to give yourself the most joyous experience.

Joy. In several regions of Africa, when a woman is pregnant, she must gather in the forest with other mothers and members of the community to discern the song of her baby. They all sing the song while she is giving birth so that the baby will be born well. When that baby grows up and begins their education or their career, or at any other important moments of life, they remember and sing their song. When they find their life partner, they sing a duet. When they are dying, the whole community sings their song. When a person has committed a crime, they also gather the community, place the offender in the middle and sing them their song to remind them of who they are.

In the faith-rooted organizing training process, we ask participants to reflect on which activities and experiences during their life's journey have made their heart sing. In order to be motivated by joy, it helps to reflect on and understand the deepest sources of our joy.

Joy can be an extremely powerful source of motivation. If something brings us joy, it's hard to keep us away from it. The pursuit of joy does not necessarily feed hedonism, however. One of the reasons we don't immediately recognize the usefulness of joy in motivating people to do justice is that we subconsciously see joy as a distraction; if we're enjoying something, we've stopped working at what's important. This is bad theology. We serve a God who wants to meet the desires of our hearts (Psalm 37:4); why would we think, then, that joy is the enemy of service? On the contrary, Rev. Frederick Buechner defines vocation as "the place where your deep gladness and the world's deep hunger meet."[7] In faith-rooted organizing we identify the sources of our joy, and then we identify that sweet spot where our joy is connected with an activity that heals the world.

Legacy. In the apostle Paul's second letter to Timothy, Timothy is reminded that his faith first dwelt in his grandmother and then in his mother. The gift that is in him came from Paul's laying on of hands. We are not merely individuals. And so we can be motivated by a legacy, a charge handed down by our elders.

A young Muslim leader heard about self-interest as a strategy for motivating participation. He responded bemusedly, "What forms the self?" We are both individual and collective beings, members of families and communities. To motivate someone, it helps to know who they are as a collective self, as someone carrying down a legacy—even a "negative" legacy from an elder they are determined not to follow.

Older people are also motivated by the legacy they want to leave behind. We want to be heroes for our children and grandchildren; even more important, we want them to live in ways that are pleasing to God and a blessing to the world.

Divine mandates. Serious Christians, Muslims and Jews are directly motivated by the *injunctions* of their faith traditions. Christians, for example, often talk in terms of the connection between faith and justice found in Scripture. Muslims speak of surrender to God's will. Jews talk about personal responsibility, particularly the responsibility to heal the world. Over the centuries, people have sacrificed and died for their faith. We should never underestimate the power of faith to move people, particularly when it is combined with the power of love and other deep sources of motivation in the soul.

Organizers who want to truly understand spiritual motivation must listen deeply to each member of the congregation or community they want to move, paying strategic attention to the way that the Spirit is moving in each heart and life, and fan the flame as appropriate.

In order to be successful at that task, every organizer has to first know his or her own complex set of core motivations. Faith-rooted organizers are trained to identify the deepest motivating forces in their own and others' souls, those forces which can overcome all of the negativity, cynicism, distraction and resistance which the larger society supports and encourages.

The Difference Between Strategic Conversation and Manipulation

The process of recruitment involves strategic conversation—conversation that has a larger purpose than simple dialogue. Unfortunately a conversation with an agenda can often feel like manipulation; in fact, it can easily *become* manipulation. Faith-rooted organizing works hard at discerning the difference between strategic conversation and manipulation.

Most of us have experienced strategic conversations that don't feel like manipulation. Therapy is an example of strategic conversation, as is education. At their best, evangelism and discipleship are forms of strategic conversation—and, as one young training participant noted, sometimes even a date can be a strategic conversation.

Strategic conversation presumes that the agenda of the one guiding the conversation matches the agenda of the other; as such, the guided conversation will benefit the other. Assuming that people often have mixed desires, strategic conversation seeks to ally itself with the healthiest and most life-giving desires in the other. We believe, as people of faith, that there is much in us that resists that which is best for us. As Paul says in the letter to the Romans, "I do not understand my own actions. For I do not do what I want, but I do the very thing I hate" (Romans 7:15 NRSV). We need strategic conversations with one another—exhortation, encouragement and the like—in order to realize our full potential for blessing and being blessed.

Jesus was a master of strategic conversation. In his dialogue with the Samaritan woman at the well (John 4), for example, he engages in a conversational dance, and he never stops speaking to the woman's heart, leading her into an increasingly profound revelation about herself and her calling.

Manipulation is a corrupted form of strategic conversation. Such conversation is guided by someone with no interest in the agenda of the other, not even concern for that person's benefit. Only the agenda of the one guiding the conversation matters. Ethical strategic conversation ultimately takes no for an answer, if that is the clear will of the other. Manipulation, on the other hand, never gives up.

Strategic conversation is always more effective than manipulation— even when it seems to result in a person's rejection of the organizer's vision. When a leader in an economic justice campaign had a conversion experience in a Pentecostal church, she stopped attending the meetings of the organization. One of the organizers asked a local pastor to remind her of her call to justice. The pastor entered into a strategic conversation with the woman; he sat with her and listened deeply to her exhaustion, her need for spiritual renewal. The Pastor told the organizer to give the woman her sabbath rest; he promised she would come back even stronger when she was ready. The organizer was initially furious over this apparent betrayal, but much to his surprise, the woman later returned as a much wiser and stronger leader.

I (Alexia) once asked the executive director of a major denominational institution to sign a letter supporting a worker justice campaign. Unbeknownst to me, his organization was facing a labor battle, and his supervisor told him he would be fired if he signed the letter. When he stopped returning my calls, instead of pressuring him I wrote him a note, thanking him for his commitment to justice and asking him to be on a panel for a set of hearings on a much safer economic justice issue. He happily came to the hearing and listened to testimony from low-wage workers in the community. I assured him that we were grateful for whatever he could contribute, and his face changed. "I'll sign the letter," he said. It was a moment of faith and courage that would not have happened had I not rejected manipulation as a way of engaging him.

The art of organizing is like the art of fishing. Both require risk and investment. At the same time that we help people to find a way to do justice joyfully, we also find appropriate ways to stretch people, to invite them into risks that make them grow. We all can acknowledge that some of the people we most treasure are those who have cared about us enough to provoke us to grow. After pushing two different clergy over a period of time to take risks, I (Alexia) received two of the most important acknowledgments of my life. One, a Jewish teacher of Torah, told me I was a *shalicha*—a messenger of God sent to bless people with the opportunity to obey God's call. The other, a Lutheran pastor from an affluent area, called me "hound of heaven"; he had avoided my phone calls for some time but was now grateful I had not stopped calling. In this role of pursuer and provoker organizers become spiritual directors for the people they are recruiting, helping them to take their next step of discipleship.

Like other models of organizing, faith-rooted organizing understands and practices the fine art of motivation. Its uniqueness is this: through strategic conversation, faith-rooted organizers pay attention to engage all the chords of the heart and soul particular to each individual, never manipulating but always pursuing. In this way faith-rooted organizers take up a call similar to that given by Jesus to Peter: "Don't be afraid; from now on you will fish for people" (Luke 5:10).

• • •

Dear Alina and Yehsong:

Most people of faith want in the depths of their souls to engage in the struggle for justice. The Holy Spirit is moving in their hearts, pushing and prodding them in that direction. Your job is to listen with your heart, understanding all that holds them back and discerning the best way to fan the flame.

Dear Alina and Yehsong, in your organizing, exercise the art of fishing with integrity and power.

10

Developing the Body of Christ

On the wall over my (Alexia's) desk hangs a postcard with the following saying:

> We do not need a leader to get us out of this mess; we need a thousand leaders.

It is not enough to get people off their couches and out the door if they don't know what to do next. Participants in the struggle for justice need to be equipped with the information and skills necessary to the task. We must develop effective leaders in order to meet our goals for community change.

Every organizing model has a set of criteria for selecting leaders, as well as a job description and a set of characteristics and capacities leaders must have in order to be effective. In most U.S.-based organizing efforts, these lists are comparable with equivalent criteria in the corporate world: leaders are articulate, assertive and analytical. They have "take charge" personalities and boundless energy, confidence, optimism and charisma—with a pinch of ruthlessness when necessary. In faith-rooted organizing, we seek to ground our understanding of leadership differently. The leaders we find in the Old and New Testament Scriptures rarely resemble those people so often rewarded with leadership positions in our day.

Leaders in Scripture are incredibly diverse in their personalities, characteristics and roles. The apostle Peter was impulsive; James was conservative; Paul was a maverick who ignored agreements when he felt he had a better plan.

Biblical leaders had personality characteristics and personal histories that might have disqualified them under most secular criteria for leadership: Moses was a murderer, David was an adulterer, and Mary Magdalene had serious personal issues.

Leadership roles in the Bible varied in the kinds of personal characteristics and abilities they required: a prophet, for example, had a different skill set from that of a king or a priest.

The biblical understanding of leadership is most beautifully expressed in the concept of the body of Christ. Each part of the body has its own role to play; that role is intimately connected and coordinated with all of the others in order for the body to function well. In faith-rooted organizing we use this body image as a guide at every level of the work.

We believe the broader movement for justice will be strongest when each sector does what it does best, contributing its unique gifts rather than using the same talking points and participating in the same activities regardless of context or giftedness. Faith-rooted organizing, for example, is not meant to be implemented when organizing neighborhoods, unions or students; it is designed instead to organize faith communities to contribute our unique gifts to the larger whole. Moreover, each participant in an organizing effort may have spiritual gifts that could contribute to the overall impact of the work. When visiting a legislator, for example, the teacher can teach, the preacher inspire, the prayer warrior sit in silent prayer, the merciful one empathize, and so on. Becoming aware of each person's gifts ahead of time allows for the effective coordination of our organizing efforts.

Sometimes we have to identify new tasks that will fit the gifts and interests of the participants. We have to get creative. Musicians might sing to the city council instead of speaking. Bakers might bake bread to be used as a gift for policymakers or as a symbol for a public action. When we blessed and distributed bread to protestors as they were being taken to jail, the baker of that bread made a meaningful and distinct contribution to the action; he ultimately became more committed to the cause.

Our different personality characteristics can guide us into complementary tasks. Prophets and organizers do not play exactly the same role, nor do their tasks require the same gift. Organizers are often pragmatists; concerned first and foremost about how to get the children enough to eat, they are ready to compromise when needed and have no permanent allies or enemies. Prophets meanwhile are often idealists, uncompromising about the purity of the vision that they proclaim and pursue. The devil celebrates when we fight one another over these differences; our cause is advanced when we acknowledge and honor our different tasks and gifts. Rev. Randy Woodley says that any struggle requires both warriors and peacemakers. There is some evidence that Rev. Martin Luther King Jr. and Malcolm X, despite their seemingly incongruent messages, had a behind-the-scenes relationship of mutual respect and even some degree of coordination. In the Philippines and Central America, base Christian communities included both revolutionaries and nonviolent faith-rooted activists. Our work can be much more powerful when we recognize the diversity and complementary nature of the body of Christ in our theory, strategy and practice.

Developing Unexpected Leadership

In 1 Corinthians 12, Paul waxes eloquent about the body of Christ. He then emphasizes that the parts of the body which appear weaker or less important are often actually more important than the others. In faith-rooted organizing, we take this seriously. We might choose a younger, less-experienced, less-polished spokesperson in order to recognize their importance and develop their gifts. One such low-income worker speaking to a congregation was so nervous that she spent most of her presentation time crying. That congregation responded with greater enthusiasm and commitment to her concerns and campaign than to any of the other, more expert speakers that day.

The gifts of children. We consistently emphasize the active inclusion of young people in leadership, based on our understanding that the Holy

Spirit can and often does speak through the mouths of children.

When my (Alexia's) daughter was seven years old, she was quietly playing in the corner at a community meeting while a strategy discussion raged over her head. All of a sudden she spoke up in her little piping voice and suggested that we remember that our opponents may be frightened of us. The adults were momentarily silenced, but when the conversation picked up again, we went in a new direction.

Another time, around Christmas, when a group of workers at a prosperous hotel were struggling with projected cuts in their health insurance benefits and pay, some children came up with a novel idea. They led a march, singing Christmas carols and bringing piggy banks to the hotel management to emphasize the real costs to families of the proposed changes.

We cannot take seriously the long-range dimension of the struggle for true and full justice unless we ensure that our organizing is truly intergenerational and honors the contributions of youth and children. As we do that, we will find that our organizing is also healthier for the child inside each of us: we will take more breaks, be more imaginative, share more with each other and nurture one another.

Uncovering gifts. Faith-rooted leadership development is not just a left brain process; it is as organic as it is structured. Those who develop the leadership of others must be spiritual directors as well as trainers, gardeners as well as builders.

In the process of lifting up unlikely leaders and unusual gifts, we often find that someone resurrects a gift that had been long buried. One of our faith-rooted training exercises involves participants writing their initials on different parts of a large drawing of a body and then explaining why they identify with that part of the body. A woman from El Salvador wrote her initials on the arm and then began to cry. As a youth she had been known as a gifted artist. In the ten years that she had lived in the United States, however, she had not once drawn or painted. She worked as a housecleaner and was known only by what she could do with her arms. During our exercise she realized, for the first time, that maybe God could use her gift in his work to create a healthy community. She began to actively use her artistic skills in justice-related activities, benefiting the movement and bringing her great joy in the process.

When we take the body image seriously, we create a level of automatic democracy that discourages arrogance and encourages servant leadership. Only Jesus is the head of the body, after all. No one gets special treatment or significantly more air time. Everyone else is equally important to the success of the overall endeavor.

This commitment requires intentionality. In bilingual groups, for example, speakers of the minority language are often effectively inhibited from full participation; they sit in the corner with a translator, or they wear heavy headphones. At CLUE we developed an "echo" method of translation in which bilingual translators roamed the room, standing just behind the person speaking and translating their words simultaneously so that everyone can participate equally. This approach, by the way, also discourages extensive lecture.

At the Oakland Catholic Worker house in the 1990s, we devised a methodology for increasing active participation of all sectors. The community was composed of U.S. residents and citizens, urban refugees and refugees from the Central American countryside. The women from the countryside rarely spoke at our meetings; rural men spoke only slightly more often. These members had little experience of this kind of decision-making meeting; they felt unequipped and intimidated. So we organized a structure where the women from the countryside met first by themselves; they then brought in the rural men. By the time they arrived at the larger group meeting, they were ready to participate, and we received the full benefit of their wisdom.

The Gift of Justice

Of course, we recognize the importance of proper training for the task of organizing to be as successful as possible. We call the spiritual gift which enables a good professional organizer the gift of justice.

People with the gift of justice often report feeling the pain of others inside their own body, even from a young age. They have the experience of uncontrollable empathy with those who suffer unjustly, of feeling like they cannot rest until justice is done. Instead of seeing a tension between mercy and justice, they find that their mercy leads them to do justice as part of the compulsion to ease suffering and create joy. Interestingly, Saul Alinsky himself described the essential characteristic of a good organizer as "the abnormal imagination that sweeps him into a close identification with mankind and projects him into its plight."[1]

In Ephesians 4 we read that the purpose of spiritual gifts is the up-building of the body of Christ. Unfortunately, however, each gift easily becomes an idol. The music minister, for example, can be so in love with making beautiful music that he doesn't let the fifteen-year-old who just came to Christ out of the gang participate in the choir because he sings off key. Likewise, people with the gift of justice are often so in love with the process of attaining change that they are outraged by those who don't see the importance of the cause; in their outrage, they alienate more people than they inspire.

We all learn best from people we trust, people who love us and want the best for us. An organizer who is using the gift of justice to build up the body acts as a servant leader, finding ways to bring others into the work with bite-sized opportunities to participate and providing a ladder to increasing involvement that fits the needs and context of the congregation.

Encouraging the Gift of Justice

The leadership of a congregation needs to recognize justice as a spiritual gift in order to properly instruct people with that gift in its management and development. There are pastors with the gift of justice, but pastors without such a gift are still called to create a fertile environment for the development of those who do have that call—an environment where their leadership and message will be welcomed.

Myles Horton (1905–1990) was a faith-rooted organizer and educator who played a highly influential role in the civil rights movement. Growing up in Tennessee, Horton decided to journey north to complete graduate studies. He studied theology at Union Theological Seminary in New York City because "I had problems reconciling my religious background with the economic conditions I saw in society."[2] Seminary studies expanded his world:

If I hadn't gone to seminary my world would be much smaller. I wouldn't have gotten to know faculty and student social activists and become involved in all the issues I didn't know existed before I left Tennessee. . . . Their discussions about social change and revolution were analytically sophisticated and showed a conviction and patience that I hadn't known before. I used to eat them up and then go back to my room and read some more in order to understand what they were talking about.[3]

It was at Union Seminary that Horton was introduced to the socially engaged, politically realist theology of Reinhold Niebuhr. Through his classes in Bible and theology he discovered the social power of Jesus' teaching of the kingdom as calling for a new social order. He was also exposed to John Dewey at Columbia University, whose problem-oriented pragmatic pedagogy shaped Horton's faith-rooted model of education and organizing. Horton went on to the University of Chicago to study sociology, where he began to realize that the desired new social order demanded faith-rooted organizing. Horton learned the importance of gathering people together to form a mass movement:

I was beginning to understand that anything worth doing had to be done with other people, and to do it with other people you had to understand the social and economic forces. It didn't mean that you were less principled, but that you had to relate what you believed to the real situation. It helped me understand that you had to organize; you had to have masses of people; and that change couldn't be brought about just because somebody had made a red-hot speech and said, "Let's have a revolution!"[4]

Horton started the Highlander Folk School in 1932 to train a new generation of leaders to usher in a new social order:

We are proposing to use education as one of the instruments for bringing about a new social order. Assuming that an individual can be integrated by having his interests aroused in a great cause in which he can lose himself, our problems—individual integration, relation of the individual to a new situation, and education for a socialistic society—become one.[5]

Both the labor movement and the civil rights movement were given prophetic fire from Highlander. Many of the leaders of the civil rights movement were trained at Highlander, including Ralph Abernathy, Dr. Martin Luther King Jr., John Lewis and James Bevel. Rosa Parks trained with Horton right before her decision to keep her seat on the bus in Montgomery, Alabama. Parks said of Horton:

> Without being educated and without being able to vote I tried to be a good citizen. I did attend a workshop at the Highlander School, and I want to tell you that the only reason I don't hate every white man alive is Highlander and Myles Horton.[6]

For Horton, education and love could not be separated; he taught that any good education begins with loving people. Love did not stop with education, however. Horton's aim was to create an entire society founded on love.

> Any decent society has to be built on trust and love and the intelligent use of information and feelings. Education involves being able to practice those things as you struggle to build a decent society that can be nonviolent.[7]

A society founded on love meant educating the people on the nature of love and how we can embody it as a prophetic community. Horton's approach to organizing was holistic, with no gaps between the mind and the heart, intelligence and love, political action and compassion.

Horton's method was also active. Love was a verb that one could learn about primarily through attempting to live it. Unlike many academics and intellectuals today, Horton's social philosophy was born from the experience of living with those whom he was teaching and working with to create a more just society.

Horton's Highlander Center was centered on a maxim that he discovered while touring folk schools in Denmark: oppressed people collectively contain creativity, power and potential for liberation that is not present in each individual. We have a greater strength as a collective than we do as individual activists. The Highlander Center experimented with learner-centered educational experiences throughout the labor movement of the 1930s, the U.S. civil rights movement, and the environmental movements of the 1970s. Many of the initiatives they worked on, such as the Citizenship Schools during the civil rights movement, developed groups of engaged community members that became the foundation of major social change. Horton believed in a "bottom up" strategy.

> Instead of thinking about having an education program to change society by working with all of its segments, especially with the people in power, so that change would come from the top, I made a decision to work with people from the bottom, who could change society from the bottom. That is the basis on which I decided to concentrate on working people, many of whom were exploited doubly, by class and race.[8]

Highlander thrived because it was able to discern the spirit of movement in the nation. It began with the labor movement in the 1930s, moved with the civil rights movement in the 1950s and 1960s, and transitioned to international education in the 1980s and 1990s. One of the legacies of the Highlander Folk School is that it found a way to educate ordinary people in faith communities, labor communities and community groups alike.

Horton and Highlander's commitment has been a great inspiration for my (Peter's) own attempt to reimagine theological education from a faith-rooted perspective. On April 12, 2010, I cofounded the Micah Institute at New York Theological Seminary with Jason Fileta, national coordinator of the Micah Challenge campaign. The Micah Institute's mission is to educate faith leaders to fight poverty and injustice through faith-rooted organizing, gathering faith leaders to work together for positive social change.

The Micah Institute draws upon the action-reflection model of theological education used at New York Theological Seminary. Inspired by Paulo Freire's *Pedagogy of the Oppressed*, this model prioritizes the perspective of the poor and oppressed in theologizing. Freire grew up in dire poverty in Brazil and spent his life reimagining education from the perspective of the oppressed. His method raises consciousness in the oppressed about their plight and provides a pathway to their empowerment and liberation.

Freire referred to the classical teaching model as the "banking model": students are viewed as empty accounts to be filled up with information, transmitted to them by teachers. In contrast, Freire took seriously the knowledge students already possessed–the knowledge necessary to interpret and navigate the world around them. Overcoming the teacher-student hierarchies of Western education models, Freire sought to establish a more democratic learning community, where revolutionary friendships were nurtured toward a better world. "Liberation is praxis," Freire writes, "the action and reflection of men upon their world in order to transform it."[9]

For Freire the final goal of the liberation struggle is a more just and equitable world. His critical pedagogy demands collective action directed toward *transformation*. The action-reflection model at the heart of Freire's critical pedagogy—communities engaging in collective action and then actively reflecting on what they are doing, resulting in a kind of social knowing—has informed my education and activism in New York City. In June 2010 I began organizing faith leaders in New York City to persuade Speaker Christine C. Quinn and the New York City Council to pass the Fair Wages for New Yorkers Act. With many partners in this venture, the Living Wage NYC campaign offered the first cohort of Micah Doctor of Ministry students the opportunity to participate in a city-wide economic justice campaign. Four Micah Fellows were hired as faith-rooted organizers to persuade clergy to join this city-wide struggle.

Edison Bond, associate minister at Citadel of Praise and a doctoral candidate in the first cohort of the Micah Doctor of Ministry program, actively recruited faith leaders while also reflecting on the group dynamics of broad-based coalition. Trained as an ethnographer, he kept careful notes of what he observed in different contexts, developing institutional ethnographies of various congregations and labor unions. In addition to observing the interpersonal dynamics of the campaign, he was also able to discern and begin to understand some of the interinstitutional dynamics of the campaign. While there were many competing egos and agendas, Bond and the other Micah Fellows (Rev. Sekou Osagyefo, Minister Reinaldo Daniel Diaz and Rev. Anita Burson) worked hard to maintain clear communication and a strong working relationship across all involved organizations as they recruited clergy and built shared power in the faith community.

Other students in the Micah Doctor of Ministry cohort joined the Micah Fellows in a silent prayer march to City Hall, and at mass meetings at several churches. Members of the city council were invited to these church meetings so they would see that faith leaders across the city were committed to the establishment of living wages. The huge crowds in churches throughout the boroughs sent a ripple effect through the city council, which voted overwhelmingly to override Mayor Michael Bloomberg's veto and ensure that the Fair Wages for New Yorkers Act would become law on June 28, 2012.

While the legislative victory was an important political breakthrough, more significantly, a citywide faith-rooted movement for economic justice was birthed. The clergy in the campaign became a cohesive learning community. Faith leaders continue to meet monthly for lunch to discern the next steps. New organizations, such as Faith in New York (a PICO affiliate led by the visionary Joseph McKellar) grew out of the living wage struggle.

Faith-rooted organizing brings together prophetic education and social action. As Martin Luther King Jr. says, "Education without social action is one-sided value because it has no true power potential. Social action without education is a weak expression of pure energy."[10] It is through the combination of the two that the vitality of the movement is created and sustained.

The action-reflection model of education works in an ongoing ebb and flow—action, reflection, action, reflection. It is almost like the Christian dialect of death, resurrection, death, resurrection. This is the heart beat of life. The Epistle of James calls us to be "doers of the Word," while St. Paul calls us to study to show ourselves approved (2 Timothy 2:15). A faith-rooted organizer worth their salt is both a deep theologian and fiery activist.

Particular Needs and Opportunities

One of the great gifts of faith communities is our emphasis on the whole person in the whole family in the whole community. We know that the psychological, spiritual and physical health of our leaders and their relationships matters for the work we do together. Faith communities also call for and honor confession, the telling of uncomfortable truths about ourselves. Becoming a faith-rooted leader in the movement for justice involves different challenges for those with a personal history of poverty and marginalization, for example, than for those who have been raised with privilege. We can and must recognize when we are internally damaged in ways that affect the work we do together.

We can admit that poverty and oppression can cause psychological and spiritual damage that make it harder to create change. We can also admit that the experience of privilege that benefits from the oppression of others is spiritually damaging in ways that also need to be directly addressed. However, if we take seriously that God has a special leadership role in mind for those who have born the direct brunt of injustice, we need in our leadership development process to prioritize healing the internal and relational damage caused by oppression.

In Manila in the early 1980s, a Belgian nun called Simone developed a clinical pastoral education program for women living in an urban squatters' area. The program adapted a curriculum typically used to train seminarians to be chaplains in hospitals and prisons; squatters were trained to provide emotional and spiritual support for their neighbors.

Unexpectedly, these newly trained chaplains also became organizers. They developed a pig-farming cooperative and engaged the community in public actions to resist the demolition of their shacks.

When I (Alexia) visited the project in 1984, I was immediately able to identify the peer chaplains; they were the only women we met in the narrow lanes of the squatters' area who stood straight, looked me in the eye and smiled. I was fascinated by the program's evident capacity to change both the internal and external landscapes of these women's lives. It seemed to seamlessly weave together strategies for spiritual healing, pastoral care, community-based economic development and community organizing.

After I completed seminary I raised funds from the Wheatridge Foundation to go back and study Sr. Simone's work, with the goal of identifying best practices for healing the psychological and spiritual damage produced by oppression and which perpetuates it. Sr. Simone had left by this time, but working with Rev. Tony Gomowad and Netty Gomowad of the Pastoral Care Foundation of the Philippines, we were able to reshape the project.

We based our study in the malnutrition ward of the National Children's Hospital in Quezon City, where women from the poorest areas provided daily care for their malnourished children. Boredom and depression motivated them to participate in our training program, and their objective situation ensured their attendance. We then accompanied them back to their barrios and replicated the program there. The great Peruvian theologian Fr. Gustavo Gutierrez said, "In the ultimate analysis, poverty means death; unjust and early death."[11] Poverty is dying before your time. We took that description a step further, acknowledging that poverty and oppression often prevent people from *living* at their full potential, like plants stunted by the lack of sufficient light, nutrients and space. When human beings experience this kind of stunting, a deep cry arises from the core of the soul—a cry that simultaneously bears grief, rage and terror. It is that cry that is the subjective component of the challenge of poverty.

Through the course of the project, we identified five aspects of the damage created by poverty that perpetuates it.

1. Low self-esteem. A common societal message to those who are "stunted" is that this state is their true nature. They hear that they have less and do less not because there are fewer opportunities and resources available to them but because they intrinsically *are* less. Without counter-messages from trusted authorities, this message enters the soul and results in low self-worth. The more a person lives out of this limited sense of capacity, the more they demonstrate their lack of capacity to themselves and others, which then reinforces the original message.

2. Fatalism. If being "stunted" is a person's true nature, then it follows that their limitations are inescapable and unchangeable. Any impulse to dream or attempt to achieve more than their peers can only result in frustration.

3. Cycles of denial and explosion. The cry of grief, rage and terror can be disabling. To manage daily tasks, the cry must be suppressed, where it builds internally until it finally erupts. Oppressed people often live with these cycles of denial and explosion, which complicates the process of analyzing problems and finding solutions: during periods of denial, the person ignores the problem, which interferes with a clear and comprehensive analysis; during periods of explosion, the person *becomes* the problem.

4. Crabs in a bucket—mutual sabotage. While oppressed people often develop complex systems of mutual aid, we also observed complex systems of mutual sabotage. One wise woman shared with us the story of the crabs in the bucket. Crabs don't like being in a bucket; when one tries to climb out, the others climb up its back, dragging it down in the process. A similar sabotage takes place among oppressed people and can even emerge out of love, not just competitiveness or hatred—fatalistic people don't believe that success is possible; they want to save their loved ones from the anguish of disappointment.

5. The other species dynamic. If one person is stunted by nature, then people who appear to be successful must be another species. You can utilize, resent or envy them, but you can't learn from them. The lessons wouldn't apply.

Having identified these damaging perspectives of the oppressed, we then identified a set of strategies to address the damage. We had to rebuild people's sense of personal potential, create networks of peer support and build effective bridges with people who could bring additional resources to the struggle. The model we developed was later adapted to the U.S. context, working with homeless leaders at the Berkeley Ecumenical Chaplaincy to the Homeless from 1988 to 1991, and ultimately replicated in six cities around the country.

Being filled with the cry inhibits learning. When a person is full, they can't take in, so we created opportunities for catharsis, for "emptying." This required that the participants be able to listen well. We led participants through a process of identifying their greatest experiences of listening or being listened to. We had them create a listening circle while each one shared her story. The resulting "emotional echo chamber" allowed safe space for the cry to be released. One woman, for example, might tell a story of being raped in a flat voice (she might even make jokes); the much stronger emotional reactions of the listening women would awaken the storyteller to her own actual emotional experience of the rape, and she would end up crying and raging. The supportive love coming from the group would then become a healing force. Speakers would realize not only their experiences of victimization but also their own contribution to their failures and losses. The storytelling ultimately became a time of confession; the love of the group was experienced as the authoritative pronouncement of forgiveness.

Group reflection on each story would help the storyteller to see God's presence and power in the midst of the pain, resulting not only in the storyteller's increased faith in external possibility but also in her capacity to see God working through her. One exercise was particularly helpful in this process. While it was difficult for the women initially to identify good characteristics in themselves, they had little problem naming their faults, so we asked them to name their faults and then helped them link their faults with a list of common defense mechanisms. We suggested that defense mechanisms are a kind of "shield" provided by God, instincts that enable people to survive in difficult circumstances. Then we explored how those "shields" could be turned into "swords"—how the women's survival strategies could be reimagined as accomplishment strategies. One woman, for example, would identify her silence as a defense mechanism; then she would see it positively as making space for others to speak. Another woman would reconceive her capacity to escape into fantasy as the power to create dreams with the potential to be realized. A third would identify her tendency to aggression as the foundation for courageous and constructive assertiveness.

As the women began to see themselves differently, it became necessary to confront the negative messages that threatened their new tentative self-image. We asked them to name "curses"—negative words often said to them about them, either by intimate or cultural authorities. One woman was often told by her mother that she was no good and would never amount to anything. (When we replicated the program in the United

States, a Native American woman remembered a plaque at a local store that read "The only good Injun is a dead Injun.") Participants would write down their curses, and we would read Scriptures about forgiveness and new life. Then we would burn the curses. Finally, participants would recall a blessing, from Scripture or some other authoritative source, that directly counteracted the message of the curse. One woman wrote, "You are God's beloved child, in whom he is well pleased." (The Native American woman wrote, "God don't make no junk.")

Faith-rooted organizing always takes participants through a process of identifying the lies that justify injustice and counteracting them with God's truth. For those who have internalized those lies as a final judgment on their own worth and potential, it is critical to see how these lies have held them back internally. Articulating the spiritual truths that counteract those lies is always a powerful experience of personal liberation.

The multiple biblical passages that proclaim the prioritization of the perspective of the poor for the sake of the common good proved to be powerful in changing participants' self-perceptions. Program participants in the Philippines and the United States carried their blessings in their pockets or wallets and read them several times a day for the duration of the program. We also incorporated a group blessing into our daily rituals: "You are my beloved [daughter or son]; with you I am well pleased" (Mark 1:11). Participants ultimately began to see their future differently. They started dreaming dreams and casting visions for themselves and for their communities.

Unfortunately, these beautiful moments of envisioning could sometimes produce a dangerous reaction. Hope can be terrifying for people who have suffered repeated disappointment. Participants would often act out in ways that would trigger accidents, crises and punishment. To counteract this, we developed a series of sessions that we called "laboratory," recognizing that scientists in a laboratory have to fail multiple times in order to succeed. Each participant was instructed to come up with a small, concrete objective that they would experiment at achieving until they got it right. They would report on their results to date at each laboratory session, describing the scientific lessons that had come out of their failures and how those lessons had led them to the next stage in the experimental process. Over the course of these sessions, participants would realize that failure is not an indictment or a sign of condemnation but rather a tool for progress.

As the participants grew in their capacity and confidence, they became ready to take on more important goals. We took the discernment process seriously, using another exercise involving a structured fantasy to arrive at a felt sense of the next step toward their goals. By experiencing that their goals really came from their own depths, participants were more able to keep going in the face of increasing difficulty.

At this point, the group began to take on common goals, moving out together to address problems common to all of them. This required new ways of working together that replaced sabotage with support. We began to establish these new patterns by asking the group to come up with examples of sabotage, discussing how these could have been turned into supportive interactions, and then role-playing both the destructive and supportive versions. (This process was often hilarious.) We then organized a daylong retreat in which each person listened to the others identify the gifts, strengths and beautiful characteristics they had observed in her. The person then shared her own weaknesses and struggles, and the group practiced responding in constructive and supportive ways.

As the program went on, the group began to become a functional and relatively healthy family. In Berkeley, where the participants all started out homeless, they began to refer to themselves as "houseless" but not "homeless"; the supportive community that we had built together had become their home.

Healing the Inner Damage Caused by Privilege

In the Philippines, we did not have the opportunity to experiment with overcoming the "other species" dynamic. However, in the United States we had a number of non-homeless volunteers who wanted to partner with the homeless peer chaplains. This created the context for exercises that enabled people with a history of oppression and people with a history of privilege to see their commonalities and to learn from and with each other. The most effective exercise was simple: people sat down in pairs to share childhood fears and hopes, experiences of grief and loss, favorite movies and music, and spiritual journeys. They then introduced each other to the group. The revelatory moments often had to do with experiences of addiction and abuse, which cut across all social classes and levels of societal power, as well as experiences of the common sacred ground of spiritual healing and prayer. The "other species" exercises ultimately addressed not only the damage caused by oppression, but also the damage caused by privilege.

Jesus said that it is as hard for a rich man to enter heaven as for a camel to go through the eye of a needle. Privilege creates spiritual and psychological damage that must be healed in order for people to bring their full contribution to God's work for justice. While I (Alexia) did not spend several years in concentrated research on that task, it has been a perennial component of my work over the past thirty-five years. The core of that damage is parallel to the "stunting" experience of the oppressed.

People who are raised with privilege receive the message in multiple ways that they are more worthy of blessing than others. This naturally leads to spiritual pride, which gets in the way of an accurate understanding of both their place in the universe and their need for God.

Privilege emphasizes wisdom that divides over wise love that unites. It encourages the tendency to unfair judgment, which carries a serious cosmic cost. Rabbi Leonard Beerman says that "our society teaches us to be dissatisfied with what we have but satisfied with what we are. Our faith teaches us to be satisfied with what we have but dissatisfied with what we are."[12] Privilege thus strengthens the spiritual sickness of our society.

In my experience, the inner damage caused by privilege is best addressed by the combination of Scripture and experience. Those who are privileged need to experience the perspective of the oppressed in order to truly understand the problem and its solution. While deep transformation requires multiple experiences and an extended period of time, even a short-term experience, if properly designed, can create powerful transformation.

In 1974, I went on one of the first Urban Plunges organized by Inter-Varsity Christian Fellowship. It was advertised as a week-long training program for students interested in urban ministry. We arrived in San Francisco and, after learning the history of ministry in the city, were told that we would be leaving the next day in pairs. We would not have our wallets or our luggage, and we would have to live on the streets for several days. We were given packets of index cards with instructions for specific activities, such as panhandling on particular street corners, or searching for food, shelter or employment. One card told us to consider selling a pint of blood for $7. (One card had an emergency phone number, with a dime attached for the pay phone.) After our sojourn on the street, we came back, cleaned up and shared our stories. Then we went back, dressed as university students, to the urban ministries and social service agencies we had previously encountered as clients. They didn't recognize any of us, and their descriptions of their services often varied widely from our experiences.

The last day of the week, we went to the tourist areas of town. I remember walking through the luxurious St. Francis Hotel; one of us discovered that the hotel had printed its monogram in the sand in the public ashtrays. We quietly began to mess up as many of the monogrammed ashtrays as we could find.

While I had grown up with a certain level of working poverty and had been on the street before as a young hippie, this experience was profoundly educational for me. I remember the generosity of poor elderly people we met in the ghetto, the disrespect shown to us by young people who would have identified with us in our normal roles. I understood how much even my relative privilege as a child had opened doors for me that would have been otherwise shut. (The plunge was even more powerful for those whose racial and economic level of privilege had been far higher than mine.) I was reminded of a study we had read in school about a couple of psychiatrists who checked themselves into a mental hospital pretending to be patients; two weeks later they had real trouble convincing the staff they were actually psychiatrists.

Creating a Community of Faith-Rooted Leaders

Whether we start out more oppressed or more privileged, we need to arrive at a common understanding of, commitment to and experience of a different kind of democracy and mutual care than our society offers. We have to build a team of leaders with the skills and discipline to support one another and share life in a way that is truly alternative to the way of the world. This is the incubator in which the new world is built; without it the results of our organizing will be just a slightly improved version of the world we start out with.

Inspired by the Native American Harmony Way, Randy Woodley calls this alternative understanding and communal practice the "Shalom Way." He experienced it in his reservation as a child—tangible spirituality, generous hospitality, extended family, diversity in the unity. "No one on the reservation is homeless," Rev. Woodley says. "Women are sacred, children are sacred, elders are respected." This theme of our deep interconnectedness is a central theological foundation for faith-rooted organizing. We build beloved community because we are part of the community of creation.

Leaders of the great movements of the twentieth century give powerful descriptions of the Shalom Way. Charlie Sherrod's story, for example, illustrates the Shalom Way at work in the American South during the civil rights movement:

> My comrades, me, Charlie Jones, Cordell Regan, some of the young people, including some of the young people from the gangs who came to work with us, chose to be non-violent. Now every day we had to decide how to live. The adults may bring us one meal but we got to decide who's going to get a haircut. How are we going to get a haircut? How are we going to get soap? How are we going to go to another city on this one little broken down car we got? We chose to work together, 10 or 15 of us down here in Southern Georgia. We couldn't expect the local people to give us everything that we needed. We had to raise some money in the north and come by some things and share that little bit that we raised, because we had some groups in Alabama, Mississippi, Florida . . . 4 or 5 groups. If I took everything myself then it would all be about me. But if I share it among the group . . . The group concept is a Christian concept. That's how Jesus worked with the disciples, all from a common fund.

We lived together under one roof for about four or five years until they burned our house down. They burned our house and almost took my wife. She was in bed pregnant and there was a young boy in the house and he knocked on the door and said there was smoke, some white people had visited the house looking for me and they set the house on fire. And at that time there were 16 of us living in this one house. We ate breakfast together, we ate lunch together when we had it and we ate dinner together. So everything was done together and we shared as much as we could share, even toothpaste sometimes. But it went further because we were able and willing to share. Like Jesus and his group, sharing things in common caused them to do things in a certain way, in a loving way, it teaches you, you see? Here we got two chairs here. Who's going to sit in the chairs, we don't have but two? It demands sharing if you set it up that way. It teaches sharing. And then the sharing becomes part of you. And it leads to the way we make decisions. If we make a decision together and here's one person not for it, he's just not for it. . . . We made decisions taking hours to make where some other folk would just take a vote. But they gone pouting after. When we leave the room we leave hugging and when we done we get back together. We leave loving. We leave everybody straight. And the guy who was so adamantly opposed, he got his way out, we figured out some kind of way to please him. And that's our total lifestyle. The way we talked to somebody, the way we shared, the way we make a decision, the way we feed each other. We wouldn't dare eat with everybody not there. See one thing leads to another. This is a law of love. You see it's law. You can't do it otherwise. And you can't tell nobody you can't do it. Everybody gonna say, "Well, well, where's Sherrod? We can't eat before Sherrod gets here. We're not going to eat and we can't start the meeting without prayer."[13]

Dolores Huerta's story from United Farmworkers illustrates a similar Shalom Way:

Thinking about people who want to start the justice walk and get on that path to justice and knowing how scary that can be, especially when you think of not following the usual path to riches and materialism, one's faith gets tested. "Am I making the right decision? Am I going the right way?" For young people who have been to college and their parents have paid for their college expecting them to become professionals and earn a lot of money and they decide, "No, I am going to do this other thing instead—I am going to work for the poor," and there's no money in it. It's a poor path. Cesar was very strong about that. He never wanted any of us in the union to earn more than the farmworkers did. And so this is why we lived off of donations and stipends because it really worked, it really created a movement. . . . Such a difference in terms of the spirit, of the way that people look at the work that they do. And Cesar, he really encouraged everyone to fast. When people fast it gives you a lot of strength as individuals. The spiritual force that comes from it makes other things happen. . . . And you know that non-violence has this rippling effect and the people who are trying to harm you are going to be affected one way or the other in their hearts or in their minds. We were picketing at the police terminal in Los Angeles and some of these Teamsters would come in and put these grape boxes on these dollies and they would just push these dollies and hit the young women in the legs with them. And these young women would just stand there and just take these hard hits of iron on their legs but they wouldn't move. And after a while the Teamsters gave up. They just could not keep doing it. And we did a march in July and August, the hottest time of the year, and we marched from Merced to Sacramento, about 150 miles. I had just had an aneurism and was recuperating. And so when he called me to the march I said, "Yes," and my family said, "Oh God, how are you going to do this march? You are just recuperating from having this aneurism." And I thought that maybe it was one of those instances when it's not very smart to do this but I felt so strongly that I had to do it. And you know I did this march and I did not get one blister, not even one. This I think encompasses a form of faith.[14]

The Shalom Way is a witness in the same way that our organizing is a witness. Faith-rooted leadership development is not merely concerned about building skills or even just individual character. We build a team of leaders with a spiritual culture that exudes the Shalom Way we are trying to bring to the world. If there is not justice in the process, there will not be the fullness of God's justice in the end—even in the benchmark ends that we set. The external manifestation of disciplined love and sacrifice also must be connected to an internal transformation.

Huerta emphasized the way that leaders in the farmworker movement were trained to be sensitive to and trust the movement of the Spirit.

> Having faith is knowing that what we do is going to have results—even when so often I can't see those results and often it may seem that I'm treading water, not getting anywhere, like when we had been on strike from 1965 going into 1970. But you know, and even if you don't know how it's going to happen, that's what faith is, you just start on that path and then the doors open up. It's like you are going out there blindfolded on this swamp and you're hoping that you're going to find the right stones to step on as you are going through this swamp blindfolded. It's testing your calling or your faith. Don't worry about making mistakes; you can always go in a different direction and learn from your mistakes. What makes us keep that faith is doing meditation, constantly questioning our own selves until we are really sure. And if it turns out to be the wrong strategy it's because we had to learn something along the way. And even if your faith is going to be disappointed in many respects because people that you trusted and had faith in fail you, or try to harm you, you learn from them anyway because they are put there in your path for some reason. So if we understand that then we don't have that hatred or anger against those individuals.[15]

In this respect, faith—like nonviolence, according to James M. Lawson Jr.—is not a tactic but a way of life. Faith-rooted leaders enter into this nonviolent, faithful way of life, not only as individuals but in their organizational and communal activities. Faith-rooted organizing develops a different array of leaders for a wide variety of leadership roles, intimately connected and coordinated like a body, all involved in a common pursuit of the Shalom Way for themselves and those around them.

●　●　●

Dear Alina and Yehsong:

To build a movement, you have to equip people to lead, each in their own way. You need to discern the gifts and calling of each and how they can best work together as a team.

The contribution of faith communities to the larger movement also includes an alternative way of being a holistic and sacrificially dedicated community of leaders. If you want to teach it, you have to be first committed to live it yourselves.

11

Prophetic Spirituality

Sustaining the Struggle

Why should I feel discouraged,
Why should the shadows come,
Why should my heart feel lonely,
And long for Heav'n and home,
When Jesus is my portion?
A constant Friend is He:
His eye is on the sparrow,
And I know He watches over me;
His eye is on the sparrow,
And I know He watches me.

TRADITIONAL CHRISTIAN HYMN

In the late 1970s, I (Alexia) worked as a campus ministry associate at the University of California in Santa Cruz. One of our projects involved organizing farmworkers, students and local church members into a collective to help provide emergency and development assistance to farmworker families. Otelia was a key leader in the project. She came from rural Mexico, where she had no formal education. She and her thirteen children lived in one room in a former army barracks. Her husband was often gone long hours in the fields. On paydays he sometimes returned empty-handed, either because the owner had not paid the workers that week or because he had gambled or drunk it away.

Otelia was a laughing soul, given to silly jokes and teasing. Once she discovered it was possible to work with her neighbors to create changes in their common life, she was famous for enthusiasm and persistence in the struggle. One day we were driving through the fields on errands, and I was fretting over being late to an appointment. I explained to Otelia that I had to go and see my friends get arrested at the Lawrence Laboratories at UC-Berkeley, where they were protesting preparations for nuclear war. Otelia was bewildered; she had never heard of nuclear weapons. By the time I was done explaining, we were both weeping with despair. She kept asking, "Are you sure that these weapons would kill everyone? All the men? All the women? All the children? All the animals? All the trees and flowers?"

When we had run out of tears, Otelia took my hand and pointed up at some birds flying in a V-formation. "Look," she said. "God will not let this happen." Then she asked me to take her home. "I am going to make tamales for you to take to your friends in jail."

Rev. James M. Lawson Jr. says that we do not have a movement for justice in the United States. Many people in many places and times are working for justice, but our communities and our society are still unjust and unhealthy in many ways. If we face the full reality of the ecological and military threats that we face, we can be completely drained by despair.

Living in denial, however, also weakens us. It leads us to avoid facing the urgency of the need to participate in public decision-making and the struggle for justice. And of course, many of us do not participate in any meaningful way. Our democracy is not fully functioning; the average person is still not engaged as a participant in creating the kind of community that they want to live in.

Traditional models of organizing do not make it easy for the average person to participate. The demands are very high, and burnout—for organizers and leaders alike—is common, bordering on inevitable. Even more, the very situation that calls for change also prevents it. Our world has seen growth in political democracy but the increasing consolidation of economic power. Most of us are more free politically but more chained economically, working harder and harder just to survive and to sustain our families. People working long hours and multiple jobs have little time left for civic participation.

We do not have a movement for justice, Lawson tells us. Rather, we have the seeds of a movement. Addressing problems that are this fundamental and global will take generations of sustained struggle. Faith communities have thousands of years of expertise in helping people to overcome discouragement and renew their commitment—the sort of expertise that can help bring these seeds to fruition.

Otelia is a witness to how we might face despair and end up with faith that creates courage and fuels commitment. How do we, as people of faith, rally the expertise of our traditions and the resources of our faith to the organizing process? What disciplines, practices, rituals and activities do we incorporate into our organizing?

CLUE LA had a weekly meeting for summer interns to go over their work plans. We realized, though, that to actually do our training and supervision as if we meant what we taught, we needed to set an additional meeting per week that focused on spiritual guidance and sustenance. And that additional meeting needed to be followed by a time of individual quiet reflection. The tone and quality of our organizing changed when we dedicated time and attention to the nurture of our faith.

When we intentionally bring our contemplative practices and perspectives to the organizing process, we see experiences of failure in a different light. In Pasadena, a group of faith leaders were accompanying mental health workers in their struggle for living wages and a greater voice in the decisions around patient care. The owners of the large non-profit health care agency they worked for had figured out an effective way to stop their campaign, and the workers were ashamed to tell the faith leaders about their defeat. Rather than immediately brainstorming next steps, the faith leaders shifted gears and drew on a different set of skills: the capacity to comfort and console the grieving. They helped the mental health workers to accept their loss and find their way to authentic hope.

One of the beautiful paradoxes of our faith is that acceptance of what is does not erase hope for what can be. As a chaplain in the Philippines and as a pastor for migrant farmworkers, I (Alexia) learned that loss is inescapable. The kind of deep acceptance that allows for the free flow of tears mystically leads to rejuvenation and new energy. The heart is watered and new sprouts grow.

Loss can also strengthen our sense of freedom. An elderly member of a primarily African American congregation in Oakland, California, once remarked on the panic experienced by many of the families in the church as they confronted an economic recession. "I know how to be poor," she said. "It doesn't stop me."

Recall the old parable about the saint and the thief. A thief hears that the holy man of the mountain has one of the most beautiful diamonds in existence. The thief determines to steal it. He sneaks into the old man's hut, finds the diamond and prepares to flee when the old man suddenly enters. The thief is about to strike him, but the old man laughs and tells him to go ahead and take the diamond. Halfway down the mountain the thief turns around. He returns and hands the diamond back to the holy man, saying, "Give me instead whatever you have that allowed you to give me this diamond so freely and joyfully." When our experience of loss and failure is planted in the fertile soil of faith, we become spiritually stronger and gain greater independence from immediate satisfaction. We are more able to fight the good fight with enduring wisdom.

Drawing from the Well

The great leaders of our faith have invariably been people of prayer and contemplation. Martin Luther is rumored to have said that he had so much to do one day that he had to pray an extra hour in the morning. In many congregations and communions, however, we separate into contemplatives and activists, and we set about arguing about which is more important to the life of faith.

In truth, we all need times of sabbath to renew our energy and center ourselves in our connection with God. Intentional meditative exercises can be excellent tools for going deeper in our prayer lives. At times of transition, I (Alexia) often take trainees through a "waking dream" in which they imagine themselves climbing a mountain. They meet someone awaiting them in a cave, who gives them a gift to take back with them. When the participants share their stories, they often find that they have a message from God that moves, inspires and renews their commitment.

We can also draw inspiration from the great cloud of witnesses that surrounds us, particularly those who have done justice as part of their walk of faith. Immersing ourselves in the stories of their lives can provide us with examples that instruct and inspire. *The Gospel at Solentiname* is a transcript of Bible studies with Nicaraguan peasants engaged in a daily struggle for justice. Reading a book like this devotionally is in itself an act of taking in sustenance for the work of justice. A number of Bible study guides are similarly rooted in the context of struggles for justice: *Reading the Bible with the Damned* by Bob Ekblad, an excellent overview of Bible studies with prisoners, lifts up interpretations of Scripture that profoundly integrate justice.[1] The LifeGuide series of Bible studies by InterVarsity Press includes books that speak to the connection between faith and justice, supporting those who seek to integrate and provide spiritual fuel for their struggles.

Even though there are thousands of Scripture passages that can strengthen and sustain us for the struggle, it's worth lifting up a few that we have found over the years to be centrally important for sustaining the work for justice. Some (such as Isaiah 58; Hebrews 13:2; Leviticus 19 and Luke 4:16-20) are explicit calls to justice. Many, however, are not typically associated with justice. Rev. Sherrod's testimony about Romans 8 reflects the experiences of many faith-rooted organizing leaders:

> It wasn't my first time ever reading the 8th chapter of Romans but that day it just looked like it opened up for me a whole new understanding of the Bible. It just penetrated me and it allowed me to deal with death—life and death. Before then I could have been scared out of my wits but after then I was bad. I was ready for Albany. I was

ready. And so going into Albany, I went without fear, without fear of death. So I was free.[2]

Hebrews 11–12 is also particularly well suited to lifting up and empowering faith-rooted organizers for the long haul.

In 2002, at the UNITE HERE (the hotel workers' union) we organized a weekly "Inspiration Group" for labor organizers. Local clergy came each week for three weeks to lead our sessions, which always included reflection on Scripture. As part of the curriculum, organizers were asked to share the Scriptures that had been most important in their lives. This simple question created an "exchange of treasures" that edified and nurtured the whole group.

Feeding the Soul

Psychologist Thomas Moore speaks about the need to cultivate not only our spirit but also our soul—the part of us that experiences spirituality in incarnate and embodied ways. We need sweet communion with those whom we love and who love us. We need times of laughter, deep sleep, good food and exercise in the outdoors. Cory Beals talks about the need to literally go out into the wilderness. Rabbi Arthur Waskow notes that all of the leaders of twentieth-century movements who have continued to support the movement for justice have stayed rooted in local communities, where they experience shared struggle and shared joy. All this feeds the soul.

The arts are also an ancient source of renewal. Creativity utilizing any artistic medium is an inspiring exercise that nurtures the soul. As we tell each other our stories as eloquently as we can, we hear in the echo chamber of our conversation that there is beauty in the pain, joy in the struggle, hope in the midst of despair, and humor in it all. This is even more powerful and tangible when our stories are sung. The one who sings, so the saying goes, prays twice.

Rev. Sherrod began our interview with him by singing a gospel song, before sharing several stories about the role of music in the civil rights movement.

The chain gang in South Carolina was perhaps up to that point the most difficult time that I had with police and with the structure of power in the south. We were making pipes, concrete pipes with machines. You go to put your hand on the machine and guide the pipe and stoop the pipe and fold and mold the pipe. But when we put our hands on the metal one day, they somehow had taken away some of the circuitry and it was shocking us. And they would be hollering at us, "Nigger" this and "Nigger" the other and "Get on with the work," you know, "You lazy son of a so-and-so," and all these kind of taunts. And that wasn't real nice with the shocks, but we did it for four hours straight. So after every time we were making pipes, we would go back to the dorm where we stayed. And at that dorm then first thing we'd do is to sit at those tables and we started singing,

> Ain't gonna let nobody Lordy, turn me 'round,
> Oh no, turn me 'round,
> Oh no, turn me 'round,
> Ain't gonna let nobody Lordy turn me 'round,
> I'm gonna keep on walking, keep on talking,
> Marching up to freedom land.

And we sang songs like that. We weren't entertaining nobody. These songs were to give us strength to meet the next day. Cause the next day it was going to be in the gutter, getting shocked or throwing that sand. But then there was a reaction from the jailers. And they were telling us, if we don't stop that "God damn singing," and "that God damn praying," and "that God damn, God damn," always "God damn." And we would keep on singing and we would keep on praying and we'd keep on testifying about the day and what we were going to do tomorrow and it was going to be an even better day tomorrow. So they put us in what they called the hole. The hole was just a very small place 'bout from that window to this side of the door, about this much area. And they put thirteen of us in a place with two bunks and a mattress, and we made do with those. We lived in the hole for three days on bread and water. And when we left the hole on the third day, we went right back to that same table and we started singing, "Can't let nobody." And we started singing, and we sang and we sang, and the jailer got upset and put us back in the hole. We went back in the hole for another three days on bread and water, and then we pushed the bread out and wouldn't eat the bread. We drank the water but we wouldn't eat the bread. And they let us out, and we kept on singing—this song "We Shall Overcome," this song that my grandma taught me twenty years before. And it just penetrated me, taught me something and made me feel deeply. And I knew where my faith is coming from and why I was so much in love with this movement.[3]

Singing has been one of the key ways of sustaining the U.S. civil rights movement. Throughout the movement, singing infused the people with hope. Through spirituals and the blues, African Americans were able to transfigure tragedy through soulful singing. In 1964, delivering the opening address to the Berlin Jazz Festival, Dr. Martin Luther King Jr. said,

The blues tell the story of life's difficulties, and if you think for a moment, you will realize that they take the hardest realities of life and put them into music, only to come out with some new hope or sense of triumph.

This is triumphant music.[4]

The freedom songs that transfigure tragedy into triumph were birthed in communities where artists and activists came together. "We Shall Overcome," the anthem of the civil rights movement, was refined into its final form at the Highlander Folk School in Tennessee. The original song, "We Will Overcome," came to Highlander from the picket line at the American Tobacco Company in Charleston, South Carolina. Pete Seeger, a Highlander musician, changed the title to "We Shall Overcome," and a group of students (who later became core leaders of SNCC) wrote new verses for the song at a Highlander workshop. Seeger, Guy and Candie Carawan, Fannie Lou Hamer and many other singers taught the song all over the South. Songs like "We Shall Overcome" were central to the social struggle, pointing the movement toward a horizon of hope. "This Little Light of Mine," originally a children's gospel song, was introduced to the movement by Zilphia Horton, the wife of Highlander cofounder Myles

Horton. "Lift Every Voice and Sing" by James and John Johnson was adopted by the NAACP as the Black national anthem, becoming a cathartic vehicle for the black political power movement and offering hope for a prophetic, intercultural future.

Christian theologian David Ford talks about people as "singing selves."[5] We all have a song to sing, and for the movement for justice to grow and be successful, everyone needs to sing their song. Music came to life in the protests and picket lines, uniting activists in one common spirit. Learning the music of the movement is thus an important way of sustaining the struggle, as music encapsulates a creative and prophetic spirituality.

Spirituals came to life in the struggles in the fields and in the streets. Music heals the "sin-sick soul," as the old hymn says. The church is, in a way, a repository of these spiritual songs that feed our soul. Every week when we go to church we bring the pains and promises, hurts and hopes of the week into the service, but there is something about singing that goes to the heart of the matter and to the depths of the soul. The physical act of singing together, with its healing vibrations through our body, actually comforts our bodies. And the texts we sing are amplified in our hearts and minds by the melodies the composers have offered us. It is no wonder that singing played such a profound role in the civil rights movement; it offers physical, mental and spiritual comfort in a communal setting, sustaining the weary and encouraging the worn. I (Peter) like to think of the church as a musical theater of the oppressed.[6]

Brazilian playwright Augusto Boal sought to break the "fourth wall" separating actors from their audience by engaging in this theater of the oppressed; the goal is the transformation of the audience from passive spectators into "spect-actors" who will in turn seek to transform their reality. The New York City–based theater troupe Compagnia de' Colombari employs this model in their annual production, *Strangers and Other Angels,* inspired by the book of Hebrews, which says, "Do not forget to show hospitality to strangers, for by so doing some people have shown hospitality to angels without knowing it" (Hebrews 13:2). Each December Colombari's wild performance piece invades public spaces in New York City, dramatically retelling the story of the birth of Jesus. Rustic shepherds, actors and brightly winged angels mingle with strangers; re-imagined medieval mystery plays intermix with the poetry of Langston Hughes; carols are sung alongside original music; opera and gospel singers join ebullient tap-dancers and step-dancers in offering the spirit of Christmas to the city. The disruptive drama serves as a sign of hope to New Yorkers and the world. Imagine if the church offered its own musical theater of the oppressed, bringing the liturgy to the streets, making spect-actors of our neighbors. Together we can change the world.

Sustaining the Soul

Faith-rooted organizing is inherently work on the run—work that is moving, as part of a movement. But the endless work of faith-rooted orga-nizing can be exhausting. With time, activism may sap our energy and health and spirit. How do we keep the movement for love and justice going?

Practicing sabbath is important to sustaining the struggle. We need to "remember the Sabbath and keep it holy" (Exodus 20:8-11). Taking days off to rest and worship God is integral to the long term sustainability of faith-rooted organizing. Attending church every Sunday immerses us in a singing community, and it exposes us to the proclamation of the Word and the celebration of the sacrament.

We can only sustain the struggle by staying connected to God our sus-tainer. The Scriptures assure us that God never grows tired or weary (Isaiah 40:28). This is an astonishing acknowledgment: no matter how exhausted we are or how much we hurt, we know God will hold us up in our weakness. We rest in the God who never grows tired and "gives strength to the weary and increases the power of the weak" (Isaiah 40:29).

Dance can be life-giving. I (Alexia) recently returned from a trip to Senegal, Africa, where I saw first-hand the truth of an African parable: the one who talks can sing and the one who walks can dance. Song and dance were daily bread for almost everyone that I encountered. The first-century church called Jesus the Lord of the Dance and included circle dances in their liturgy. For years, I taught congregations to do folk dances to the tune of Christmas carols; I had noticed that no one who danced while singing "Joy to the World" sang it without smiling. As the great Unitarian storyteller Robert Fulghum has observed, there are no kindergartners that believe that they cannot dance, sing or paint. It is only as we grow up (in some cultures) that we are discouraged from participating in the arts because we lack talent.

Sustaining Communities

While many of the activities that congregations do together aim to sustain, heal and inspire, many such rituals and ceremonies are not linked by the congregation explicitly to the wounds and weariness experienced in the battle for justice. Throughout the ages and around the world, however, faith communities have celebrated, prayed and cared for each other in ways that have sustained and inspired the struggle for community change. I (Alexia) will never forget marching with thousands of people in the Philippines to the palace of the dictator Ferdinand Marcos, demanding democratic elections and an end to human rights abuses. At the front of the line, facing soldiers with guns, all of the pastors joined together in the celebration of the Lord's Supper, completely disregarding the denominational strictures that would have normally kept us apart. For an hour, we lost our fear in communion with Christ and one another. We need to intentionally create, research and share ways of worshiping that connect us more deeply to the call to justice if we are to sustain the struggle for a lifetime.

Children of organizers in the United States, like children of pastors, are often ambivalent about the movement that took away the time and energy of their parents. They often feel pushed aside, deprived and resentful. By contrast, my experience in both the Philippines and in Central America was that children had far less resentment toward their parents or such movements. The continuity from generation to generation was far stronger—even when parents were murdered by the forces of oppression or forced to live on the run for years. Children played where organizing meetings were held. Children made art and posters for actions. Children gave their ideas and opinions, and sometimes spoke publicly on behalf of the movement. Families were not in competition with the church or the community but rather were fed and nurtured in the context of the broader work. Meetings and events were structured accordingly; far more time was given to eating together, to making music, to telling funny and sad stories, to sharing lives, to laughing at the antics of children. Meetings lasted for hours to enable time for the direct work of planning and strategy development as well as time for prayer and playfulness. Cultural nights, in which everyone shared a story, song, poem or other creative act, were integrated into every retreat or conference.

For these models to flourish in a Western context, we will need to be intentional about fighting our overemphasis on individualism and returning to a more biblical balance of collective and individual selves. When my daughter did an organizing internship with a sister organization at age thirteen, she wrote in a final paper that she had gone through an angry period of wanting a normal life. She wanted to sit in front of the television for hours, to do whatever she felt like doing, instead of having to be with the church or movement. She was later grateful, however, that she had not been formed in that way but had been given a different, countercultural, understanding of life that was much closer to the biblical mandate.

Remember Hope

Faith-rooted organizing seeks not only to build leaders but to sustain leaders for generations, creating a movement with so much momentum that we realize as much of the dream as is possible in a fallen world. In the end, it is our hope which sustains us most of all. We hope in the resurrection of Jesus; we also hope in the kingdom of God—Jesus' most common theme. The kingdom of God is what happens when God's will is done fully. There will be a time when God's will is done fully. There are also and will yet be foretastes of the feast to come. The kingdom is at hand, Jesus said, and we can experience it in our midst in a multitude of ways. We know that when we pray "Your kingdom come, your will be done, on earth as it is in heaven," we are not only praying for the kingdom to be manifest *around* us but *through* us, through our words and deeds.

Yet we know that our words and deeds are always insufficient to create all of the justice we hunger for. So how do we keep on keeping on in light of that regular disappointment? Our struggle for justice is driven by patience and progress.

Theologian Teresa Delgado talks about the combination of revolutionary patience and revolutionary impatience—trying to approach perfection while accepting continual imperfection as a way of living, of being an imperfect community that channels the divine. To have a living hope is a way of life. When understood properly, it gives us enduring courage. A final word from Dolores Huerta:

> We started the big grape boycott in 1968. And then we kept coming back to Delano, you know, for board meetings. And I always felt that I didn't want to see the farmworkers because they're going to say, "Well, why haven't we won yet?" And I was kind of bracing myself and when I would see the workers, I would feel really apologetic. And they'd say, "Senora Huerta, don't worry. We are going to win next year. Don't worry, don't, we're fine, we're fine here. Just keep out there working. If we don't win this year, we'll win next year." Cesar said in the end we will win. In the end we will win. The only time you lose is when you quit. More recently, we had a woman who came in and she was just frustrated and she said, 'Why, I question this. Why should I continue to even belong to the Catholic church when all these things are happening?" And the only answer I could think of was faith. We have to have faith that people will change and organizations will change. We have to keep that faith. Once you become cynical, you give up and you can't change anything. Cesar said you can never give up. We've got to continuously have faith.[7]

Faith-rooted organizing is a vehicle for filling our organizing with as much faith as we can have. It is organizing as if God is real, Jesus is risen, and the Holy Spirit is alive in the movement.

•   •   •

Dear Alina and Yehsong:

We are depending on you to be faith-rooted organizers—each in your own way—and to carry the torch of the movement to build the beloved community down to the next generation, to your children and grandchildren.

We'll give you everything we can pass on, everything that has sustained us.

And we can't wait to see what new things God will do in and through you.

Many blessings and much love,

Alexia and Peter

Appendix

Faith-Rooted Serpent Power

When I (Alexia) first shared my growing commitment to dove power with a friend, her reaction was mixed. A nationally known faith-based organizer and social justice leader, she reminded me that many good church folk are woefully unstrategic. She was concerned that I was encouraging them essentially to be, as my grandmother would say, "so spiritual that they were no earthly good." Jesus did not call us to be only innocent as doves; he also called us to be wise as serpents.

The ultimate "wise as serpents" parable is found in Luke 18:1-5. A widow—one of the most powerless people in the ancient world—is mistreated by a judge who "does not fear God or respect people." She doesn't take no for an answer, however. She continues to advocate persistently and passionately for her cause. Finally, Jesus says, the judge agrees to grant her justice.

The judge has not changed, Jesus explains. He has not awakened to his better self. He has not undergone a conversion. He still does not respect people or fear God. He grants the widow justice, rather, because she exerts a critical mass of pressure.

This is serpent power in its essence: people overcoming institutional power (such as the power of organized money) by exercising the power they have as members of a community (the power of organized people).

So, how do we exercise serpent power faithfully?

To exercise serpent power faithfully is to recognize that we must work in coalition with those who bring other gifts and contributions to the struggle. A billboard lifting up a faith-rooted principle does very little outside a broader coalition preparing a series of actions, timed for maximum impact and designed to reinforce the message of the coalition. Each victorious struggle mentioned in this book was won by a wide variety of actions carried out by different partners—unions, corporations, political groups, community groups—all using the basic human skills of serpent-power organizing.

To exercise serpent power faithfully is to think strategically. Translate your goals into realistic, measurable objectives. Then design strategies aimed at achieving those objectives. God cares about the unity of the family; you are seeking, in obedience to his will, to maintain the unity of immigrant families. What policies in the pipeline could achieve those goals? Who is interested in those policies? What and who are they influenced by? What constituency are they accountable to? What connections provide the base of their support? What case for change would make sense to them, given their assumptions and values? What steps do you need to take in order to provide that case, bring together those constituents and influence those connections? Diagram the necessary steps to attain your goals and the resources (human and otherwise) you must pull together in order to take those steps. You can base your unity on principles instead of specific policies—but you should know which policies are viable, and your push for principles should be sufficiently strategically aligned to support good policies.

To exercise serpent power faithfully is to be conscious and nimble. The battlefield is constantly shifting. To be wise as a serpent is to be disciplined in your attention to those shifts. Are potential allies emerging? Are coalitions crumbling or forming? Where can you best contribute your gifts and the dove power that you bring? Jesus calls us to "read the signs of the times."

To exercise serpent power faithfully is to get formal training. The Midwest Academy, Labor Schools, PICO and Marshall Ganz's affiliates provide a base of serpent skills to integrate with dove power. Faith-rooted organizing trainers around the country can also be identified by contacting the authors at alexiasalvatierra.com or peterheltzel.wordpress.com.

Faith-rooted organizing calls us to truly be wise as serpents and innocent as doves, to be good stewards of all the potential power that God has given us to achieve his purposes.

Acknowledgments

We would like to thank our friends, colleagues and students at New York Theological Seminary, especially our colleagues in the Micah Doctor of Ministry program in Transformational Leadership and Faith-Rooted Organizing, Professors Wanda M. Lundy and Eleanor Moody Shepherd. Joya Colon-Berezin, Karen Blacks, Edison Bond, Daniel Reinaldo Diaz, Alexie Torres-Fleming and Leah Kozak of the Micah Institute have also been a great inspiration to our work. We are thankful for the doctoral students at New York Theological Seminary who have read and commented on a draft of this book.

We are grateful to David Zimmerman for his passionate, patient and precise work as our editor at InterVarsity Press. We would like to thank Bo Eberle, Leah Kozak and Joe Strife for their help in preparing the index.

As we have researched and written the book several people have read all or parts of it and offered us insightful comments and criticisms. They include Bo Eberle, Leah Hunt-Hendrix, Mark Lau Branson, Matthew Lyon, Peter Ochs, Christopher Smith and Joe Strife. Sandra Van Opstal gave essential emotional and spiritual support to Alexia at key moments in the process. Pastor Alvin Jackson at Park Avenue Christian Church has encouraged Peter's call to embody the spirit of the mystical-prophetic ministry of Howard Thurman and Martin Luther King Jr.

We would like to thank our friends in many organizations that we partner with, including Christian Community Development Association, Evangelicals for Justice, Faith in New York, the Federation of Poverty Welfare Workers, New York Faith and Justice, the Parish Collective, Red Letter Christians, Sojourners, PICO, World Relief and World Vision.

We would also like to thank a growing network of faculty at seminaries and Christian Colleges who are committed to faith-rooted organizing: Auburn Seminary, Biola University, Claremont School of Theology, Covenant Theological Seminary, Denver Seminary, Fuller Theological Seminary, Gordon-

Conwell Theological Seminary, New York Theological Seminary, Seattle School of Theology and Psychology, Talbot Seminary at Biola University, Union Theological Seminary (especially the Poverty Initiative) and Vanguard University.

We would like to thank the following scholars who we interviewed at the American Academy of Religion Annual Meeting in San Francisco, California, on November 19, 2012: Randy Woodley, Sharon Welch, Darby Ray, Joerg Rieger, Corey Beals, Johnny Hill, Jennifer McBride, and Teresa Delgado. We would also are grateful for interviews of Willie Baptist, Shane Claiborne, Noelle Damico, Cheri Honkala, Liz Theoharris and Alexie Torres-Fleming.

With all our hearts, we thank the members of the Council of Elders and the other elders that were interviewed for the creation of the CLUE faith-rooted website, with special gratitude for Dolores Huerta, Rev. James M. Lawson Jr., Rev. Charlie Sherrod, Rev. Phil Lawson, Rabbi Leonard Beerman, Rev. Nelson Johnson and Joyce Johnson, and Marshall Ganz. We also thank the circle of young leaders at CLUE who helped envision faith-rooted organizing: Sameerah Siddiqui, Bridie Roberts, Diana Mendoza, Alison Abrams and Paula Witt. We deeply appreciate the support and insights of a number of faith-rooted organizers around the country, including Rev. Ian Danley, Rev. Troy Jackson, Lisa Sharon Harper, Rev. Tim and Cote Soerens, Rev. Adam Taylor, Matt Soerens, Rev. Amanda Morgan, Wendy Tarr, Michelle Warren, Rev. Eileen Suico, Mary Nelson, Rev. Michael Mata, Rev. Martin Garcia, Kristn Kumpf, Rev. Sung Yeon Choi Morrow, Josh Harper, Rev. Dr. Juan Martinez, Dr. Stephen Pavey, Elder Ricardo Moreno, Rev. Walter Contreras, Rev. Keith Stewart, Rev. Wes Helms, Rev. Jennifer Kottler, Rev. Deth Im, Rev. Sean Hatch, Rev. Alan and Lydia Bean, Juan Carlos Ruiz, Maryada Vallet, Max Krueger, Rev. Ivan Gonzalez and Rev. Ric Hudgens (and many more). We also honor the memory and comradeship of Richard Twiss.

We would also like to thank our families for their love and support as we finished this book.

We would like to thank Ken Wytsma for the invitation to speak at the Justice Conference in Philadelphia on February 22-23, 2013, where we were able to finish the book in the City of Brotherly and Sisterly Love. As we heard the sound of the Liberty Bell, the symbol of America, once again, we were inspired to organize for justice and "Let Freedom Ring!"

For Further Reading

Alinsky, Saul. *Reveille for Radicals.* New York: Vintage Books, 1989.

————. *Rules for Radicals: A Pragmatic Primer for Realistic Radicals.* New York: Vintage Books, 1989.

Baptist, Willie, and Jan Rehman. *Pedagogy of the Poor: Building the Movement to End Poverty.* New York: Teachers College Press, 2011.

Benson, Bruce Ellis, Melinda Berry, and Peter Heltzel, eds. *Prophetic Evangelicals: Envisioning a Just and Peaceable Kingdom.* Grand Rapids: Eerdmans, 2012.

Blum, Edward J., and Paul Harvey. *The Color of Christ: The Son of God and the Saga of Race in America.* Chapel Hill: University of North Carolina Press, 2012.

Bonhoeffer, Dietrich. *Discipleship.* Translated by Barbara Green and Reinhard Krauss. Volume 4 of *Dietrich Bonhoeffer Works,* 16 vols. Minneapolis: Fortress Press, 2003.

————. *Letters and Papers from Prison.* Translated by Reginald Fuller et al. New York: Touchstone, 1997.

Brueggemann, Walter. *Living Toward a Vision: Biblical Reflections on Shalom.* 2nd ed. New York: United Church Press, 1982.

————. *Peace: Understanding Biblical Themes.* St. Louis: Chalice Press, 2001.

Casanova, Ron. *Each One Teach One.* Willimantic, CT: Curbstone Press, 1996.

Cavanaugh, William T. *Theopolitical Imagination.* New York: T & T Clark, 2002.

Chambers, Ed. *Roots for Radicals: Organizing for Power, Action, and Justice.* New York: Continuum, 2003.

Cone, James H. *The Spirituals and the Blues: An Interpretation.* Maryknoll, NY: Orbis, 1991.

Crockett, Clayton, and Jeffrey Robbins. *Religion, Politics and the Earth: The New Materialism*. New York: Palgrave Macmillan, 2012.

Evans, Sara M., and Harry C. Boyte. *Free Spaces: The Sources of Democratic Change in America*. Chicago: University of Chicago Press, 1992.

Fluker, Walter E. *They Looked for a City: A Comparative Analysis of the Ideal of Community in the Thought of Howard Thurman and Martin Luther King, Jr.* Lanham, MD: University Press of America, 1989.

Gilroy, Paul. *The Black Atlantic: Modernity and Double Consciousness*. Cambridge, MA: Harvard University Press, 1993.

Harper, Lisa Sharon. *Evangelical Does Not Equal Republican—or Democrat*. New York: New Press, 2008.

Heltzel, Peter Goodwin. *Jesus and Justice: Evangelicals, Race and American Politics*. New Haven, CT: Yale University Press, 2009.

———. *Resurrection City: A Theology of Improvisation*. Grand Rapids: Eerdmans, 2012.

Hendricks, Obery M., Jr. *The Politics of Jesus: Rediscovering the True Revolutionary Nature of the Teachings of Jesus and How They Have Been Corrupted*. New York: Doubleday, 2006.

———. *The Universe Bends Toward Justice: Radical Reflections on the Bible, the Church, and the Body Politic*. Maryknoll, NY: Orbis, 2011.

Horwitt, Sanford. *Let Them Call Me Rebel: Saul Alinsky—His Life and Legacy*. New York: Knopf, 1989.

Jackson, Troy. *Becoming King: Martin Luther King and the Making of a National Leader*. Lexington: University of Kentucky Press, 2008.

Jacobsen, Dennis. *Doing Justice: Congregations and Community Organizing*. Minneapolis: Fortress, 2001.

Kaylor, David R. *Jesus the Prophet: His Vision of the Kingdom on Earth*. Louisville, KY: Westminster John Knox, 1994.

King, Martin Luther, Jr. *A Testament of Hope: The Essential Writings and Speeches of Martin Luther King, Jr.* Edited by James Melvin Washington. San Francisco: HarperCollins, 1986.

———. *The Trumpet of Conscience*. New York: Harper & Row, 1968.

Lowery, R. H. *Sabbath and Jubilee*. St. Louis: Chalice Press, 2000.

MacIntyre, Alasdair. *After Virtue: A Study in Moral Theory*. Notre Dame,

IN: University of Notre Dame Press, 1981.

———. *Whose Justice? Which Rationality?* Notre Dame, IN: University of Notre Dame Press, 1988.

Marsh, Charles. *Beloved Community: How Faith Shapes Social Justice, from the Civil Rights Movement to Today.* New York: Basic Books, 2004.

Marsh, Charles, and John Perkins. *Welcoming Justice: God's Movement Toward Beloved Community.* Downers Grove, IL: InterVarsity Press, 2009.

McBride, Jennifer M. *The Church for the World: A Theology of Public Witness:* Oxford: Oxford University Press, 2012.

Meeks, M. Douglas. *God the Economist: The Doctrine of God and Political Economy.* Minneapolis: Fortress, 1989.

Moses, Greg. *Revolution of Conscience: Martin Luther King, Jr., and the Philosophy of Nonviolence.* New York: Guilford Press, 1967.

Nelson, Eric. *The Hebrew Republic.* Cambridge, MA: Harvard University Press, 2010.

North, Robert, S.J. *Sociology of Biblical Justice.* Rome: Pontifical Biblical Institute, 1954.

Rah, Soong-Chan. *The Next Evangelicalism.* Downers Grove, IL: InterVarsity Press, 2009.

Ransby, Barbara. *Ella Baker and the Black Freedom Movement: A Radical Democratic Vision.* Chapel Hill: University of North Carolina Press, 2003.

Ray, Stephen. *Do No Harm: Social Sin and Christian Responsibility.* Minneapolis: Fortress, 2002.

Reed, Adolph. *Stirrings in the Jug: Black Politics in the Post-Segregation Era.* Minneapolis: University of Minneapolis Press, 1999.

Rieger, Joerg. *No Rising Tide: Theology, Economics & the Future.* Minneapolis: Fortress, 2009.

Rivera, Ray. *Liberating the Captives.* Grand Rapids: Eerdmans, 2012.

Rorty, Richard. *Achieving Our Country: Leftist Thought in Twentieth Century America.* Cambridge, MA: Harvard University Press, 1998.

Ryan, John Augustine. *A Living Wage: Its Ethical and Economic Aspects.* New York: Macmillan, 1906.

Sider, Ron J., ed. *Cry Justice: The Bible on Hunger and Poverty.* New York: Paulist, 1980.

Slessarev-Jamir, Helen. *Prophetic Activism: Progressive Religious Justice Movements in Contemporary America.* New York: New York University Press, 2011.

Sobrino, Jon. *Jesus the Liberator: A Historical-Theological Reading of Jesus of Nazareth.* Maryknoll, NY: Orbis, 1993.

Stout, Jeffrey. *Democracy and Tradition.* Princeton, NJ: Princeton University Press, 2004.

Taylor, Adam. *Mobilizing Hope.* Downers Grove, IL: InterVarsity Press, 2009.

Thurman, Howard. *Deep River: The Negro Spiritual Speaks of Life and Death.* Richmond, IN: Friends United Press, 1975.

Trochmé, André. *Jesus and the Nonviolent Revolution.* Translated by Michael H. Shank and Marlin E. Miller. Scottdale, PA: Herald Press, 1956.

Vanhoozer, Kevin J. *The Drama of Doctrine: A Canonical-Linguistic Approach to Christian Theology.* Louisville, KY: Westminster John Knox, 2005.

Warren, Mark. *Dry Bones Rattling: Community Building to Revitalize American Democracy.* Princeton, NJ: Princeton University Press, 2001.

Wells, Samuel. *Improvisation: The Drama of Christian Ethics.* Grand Rapids: Brazos, 2004.

Wolterstorff, Nicholas. *Justice: Rights and Wrongs.* Princeton, NJ: Princeton University Press, 2008.

Woodley, Randy. *Shalom and the Community of Creation: An Indigenous Vision.* Prophetic Christianity Series, vol. 2. Grand Rapids: Eerdmans, 2012.

Wood, Richard. *Faith in Action: Religion, Race and Democratic Organizing in America.* Chicago: University of Chicago Press, 2002.

Yoder, Perry. *Shalom: The Bible's Word for Salvation, Justice, and Peace.* Nappanee, IN: Evangel Publishing, 1987.

Zucchino, David. *Myth of the Welfare Queen.* New York: Scribner, 1997.

Notes

Introduction

[1]Some faith-based organizing networks, particularly the PICO network (www.piconetwork.org) and independent networks in specific cities, have been moving toward practicing a form of faith-rooted organizing.

[2]Faith-rooted organizing is being used in the context of many different faith traditions; Jewish and Muslim groups are actively exploring ways that this model can contribute to their organizing efforts. This book, however, focuses on an evangelical Christian understanding of faith-rooted organizing.

[3]Videos of interviews with veteran faith leaders are available on CLUE-CA's website: www.cluela.org.

[4]For further discussion of the prophetic evangelical movement see Peter Goodwin Heltzel, "Prophetic Evangelicals: Toward a Politics of Hope," in *The Sleeping Giant Has Awoken: The New Politics of Religion in the United States*, ed. Jeffrey W. Robbins and Neal Magee (New York: Continuum, 2008), pp. 25-40; idem, *Jesus and Justice: Evangelicals, Race and American Politics* (New Haven, CT: Yale University Press, 2009); Soong-Chan Rah, *The Next Evangelicalism: Freeing the Church from Western Cultural Captivity* (Downers Grove, IL: InterVarsity Press, 2009). For a prophetic evangelical reflection on the central themes of Christian faith, see Bruce Ellis Benson, Malinda Berry and Peter Goodwin Heltzel, eds., *Prophetic Evangelicals: Envisioning a Just and Peaceable Kingdom* (Grand Rapids: Eerdmans, 2012). Prophetic evangelicalism has roots in the nineteenth-century abolition movement; see Timothy L. Smith, *Revivalism and Social Reform in Mid-Nineteenth-Century America* (New York: Abingdon, 1957); Donald W. Dayton, *Discovering an Evangelical Heritage* (New York: Harper & Row, 1976).

Chapter 1: The Roots of Faith-Rooted Organizing

[1]Howard Thurman best represents the mystical aspects of this struggle, with Martin Luther King Jr. best representing the prophetic aspects. But both poles were operative in each of their theologies. Our conception of mystical-prophetic theology is indebted to David Tracy's "Dialogue and the Prophetic-Mystical Option," in *Dialogue with the Other: The Inter-Religious Dialogue* (Grand Rapids: Eerdmans, 1991), pp. 95-123; cf. M. Shawn Copeland, "To Live at the Disposal of the Cross: Mystical-Political Discipleship as Christo-logical Locus," in *Christology: Memory, Inquiry, Practice,* ed. Anne M. Clifford and Anthony Godzieba (Maryknoll, NY: Orbis, 2003).

[2]Nicholas Wolterstorff, *Justice: Rights and Wrongs* (Princeton, NJ: Princeton University Press, 2008), p. 82. See Perry Yoder, *Shalom: The Bible's Word for Salvation, Justice, and Peace* (Nappanee, IN: Evangel Publishing, 1987).

[3]See, for example Lewis V. Baldwin, *Toward the Beloved Community: Martin Luther King, Jr. and South Africa* (Cleveland: Pilgrim Press, 1995); Walter E. Fluker, *They Looked for a City: A Comparative Analysis of the Ideal of Community in the Thought of Howard Thurman and Martin Luther King, Jr.* (Lanham, MD: University Press of America, 1989); Charles Marsh, *The Beloved Community: How Faith Shapes Social Justice, from the Civil Rights Movement to Today* (New York: Basic Books, 2005); and Greg Moses, *Revolution of Conscience: Martin Luther King, Jr., and the Philosophy of Nonviolence* (New York: Guilford Press, 1967).

[4]For a helpful elaboration of these two theological claims in King in conversation with personalist philosophy and Christian ethics, see Rufus Burrow Jr., *God and Human Dignity: The Personalism, Theology and Ethics of Martin Luther King, Jr.* (South Bend, IN: University of Notre Dame Press, 2006).

[5]See Ralph Luker, "The Kingdom of God and the Beloved Community in the Thought of Martin Luther King, Jr.," in *Ideas and the Civil Rights Movement,* ed. Ted Ownby (Jackson: University Press of Mississippi, 2001), pp. 39-54; cf. Peter Goodwin Heltzel, "Martin Luther King, Jr.'s Theology of the Cross," in *Jesus and Justice: Evangelicals, Race and American Politics* (New Haven, CT: Yale University Press, 2009), pp. 87-93.

[6]Martin Luther King Jr., "The American Dream," in *A Testament of Hope: The Essential Writings and Speeches of Martin Luther King, Jr.,* ed. James Melvin Washington (San Francisco: HarperCollins, 1986), p. 215.

[7]Martin Luther King Jr., *The Papers of Martin Luther King, Jr.,* vol. 3, ed. Clayborne Carson, Susan Carson, Adrienne Clay, Virginia Shadron and Kieran

Taylor (Berkeley: University of California Press, 1996), p. 136.

[8]Troy Jackson, *Becoming King; Martin Luther King and the Making of a National Leader* (Lexington: University of Kentucky Press, 2008), p. 5.

[9]King, "I Have a Dream," in *Testament of Hope,* pp. 217-20.

[10]On the unfinished legacy of Dr. King and the promise of the Poor Peoples Campaign for reconstituting a poor-led movement for global justice, see The Poverty Initiative at Union Theological Seminary, *A New and Unsettling Force: Reigniting Rev. Dr. Martin Luther King, Jr.'s Poor People's Campaign* (New York: The Poverty Initiative, 2009). Peter Goodwin Heltzel, *Resurrection City: A Theology of Improvisation* (Grand Rapids: Eerdmans, 2012), pp. 106-14; cf. Peter Heltzel, "Radical (Evangelical) Democracy: The Dreams and Nightmares of Martin Luther King, Jr. and Antonio Negri," *Political Theology* 10, no. 2 (April 2009): 287-303.

[11]Martin Luther King Jr., *The Trumpet of Conscience* (New York: Harper & Row, 1968), p. 24.

[12]On the notion of the just and peaceable kingdom see Bruce Ellis Benson, Malinda Berry and Peter Heltzel, eds., *Prophetic Evangelicals: Envisioning a Just and Peaceable Kingdom* (Grand Rapids: Eerdmans, 2012), pp. 8-30; R. David Kaylor, *Jesus the Prophet: His Vision of the Kingdom on Earth* (Louisville, KY: Westminster John Knox, 1994).

[13]For an explanation of shalom justice in the Hebrew Bible, see Heltzel, *Resurrection City*, 22-24.

[14]Obery M. Hendricks Jr., *The Politics of Jesus* (New York: Doubleday, 2006); Arland J. Hultgren, *The Parables of Jesus: A Commentary* (Grand Rapids: Eerdmans, 2000).

[15]See Charles Marsh, "The Civil Rights Movement as Theological Drama—Interpretation and Application," *Modern Theology* 18, no. 2 (April 2002): 231-50; Charles Marsh, *God's Long Summer: Stories of Faith and Civil Rights* (Princeton, NJ: Princeton University Press, 1997).

[16]Ernesto Cardenal, *The Gospel in Solentiname* (Maryknoll, NY: Orbis, 1976).

[17]George Higgins, *Organized Labor and the Church* (New York: Paulist, 1993), p. 87.

[18]Ibid., p. 91.

[19]Ibid., p. 92.

Chapter 2: Dreaming God's Dream Together

[1]Saul Alinsky, *Rules for Radicals* (New York: Vintage, 1989), p. 3.

[2]For an analysis of sin as both personal and social see Stephen Ray, *Do No Harm: Social Sin and Christian Responsibility* (Minneapolis: Fortress, 2002).

[3]Jeffrey Stout, *Blessed Are the Organized: Grassroots Democracy in America* (Princeton, NJ: Princeton University Press, 2010), p. 37.

[4]Since the American colonists immigrated from many different countries, they had to come up with a strategy to unify their ethnic and political identity. White skin color, or "whiteness," became the strategy deployed to create a normative ethnic identity in the United States. Whiteness is a fluid category, however, that would gradually expand through the history of U.S. immigration. Different ethnic groups are designated as white at different moments within American history. For example, when Irish Catholics first arrived in droves during the 1840s, they were not considered white; with time, however, they would be assimilated into what Matthew Frye Johnson calls the "alchemy of whiteness." Matthew Frye Jacobson, *Whiteness of a Different Color: European Immigrants and the Alchemy of Race* (Cambridge, MA: Harvard University Press, 1998); cf. Nell Irvin Painter, *The History of White People* (New York: W. W. Norton, 2010); David R. Roediger, *Working Toward Whiteness: How America's Immigrants Became White, The Strange Journey from Ellis Island to the Suburbs* (New York: Basic Books, 2005); Edward J. Blum and Paul Harvey, *The Color of Christ: The Son of God and the Saga of Race in America* (Chapel Hill: University of North Carolina Press, 2012).

[5]Alinsky, *Rules for Radicals,* p. 11.

[6]Stout, *Blessed Are the Organized,* p. 278.

[7]See Ron J. Sider, ed., *Cry Justice: The Bible on Hunger and Poverty* (New York: Paulist Press, 1980).

[8]For theological introductions to the biblical concept of shalom, see Walter Brueggemann, *Living Toward a Vision: Biblical Reflections on Shalom,* 2nd ed. (New York: United Church Press, 1982); Perry Yoder, *Shalom: The Bible's Word for Salvation, Justice, and Peace* (Nappanee, IN: Evangel Publishing, 1987).

[9]See Temba L. J. Mafico, "Just, Justice," *The Anchor Bible Dictionary* vol. 3, ed. David Noel Freedman (New York: Doubleday, 1992), pp. 1127-29; cf. James L. Mays, "Justice: Perspectives from the Prophetic Tradition," in *Prophecy in Israel* (Philadelphia: Fortress, 1987), pp. 144-58; Nicholas Wolterstorff, *Justice: Rights and Wrongs* (Princeton, NJ: Princeton University Press, 2008); Wolterstorff, *Justice in Love* (Grand Rapids: Eerdmans, 2011).

[10]Walter Brueggemann, *Peace: Understanding Biblical Themes* (St. Louis: Chalice Press, 2001), p. 13.

[11]Ibid., p. 18.

[12]For a more a more detailed discussion of shalom justice in the Hebrew Scripture, see Peter Heltzel, "Shalom Justice: the Prophetic Imperative," in *Resurrection City: A Theology of Improvisation* (Grand Rapids: Eerdmans, 2012), pp. 22-48.

[13]Joerg Rieger develops the idea of "deep solidarity" with Kwok Pui-Lan in *Occupy Religion* (Lanham, MD: Rowman & Littlefield, 2012), pp. 78-87, 128-33. For more theological analyses of the year of jubilee see John S. Bergsma, *The Jubilee from Leviticus to Qumran* (Leiden: Brill, 2007); R. H. Lowery, *Sabbath and Jubilee* (St. Louis: Chalice Press, 2000); M. Douglas Meeks, *God the Economist: The Doctrine of God and Political Economy* (Minneapolis: Fortress, 1989); Eric Nelson, *The Hebrew Republic* (Cambridge, MA: Harvard University Press, 2010), pp. 64-87; Robert North, S.J., *Sociology of Biblical Justice* (Rome: Pontifical Biblical Institute, 1954); and André Trochmé, *Jesus and the Nonviolent Revolution,* trans. Michael H. Shank and Marlin E. Miller (Scottdale, PA: Herald Press, 1956), pp. 48-52.

[14]For a theological analysis of the community of creation with reference to Native American theology, see Randy Woodley, *Shalom and the Community of Creation: An Indigenous Vision*, Prophetic Christianity Series, vol. 2 (Grand Rapids: Eerdmans, 2012). In this work Woodley persuasively narrates how Israel's ethic of shalom justice and Native American Harmony Way worldviews can create a new way of life for North American Christians. See Woodley's discussion of the "Harmony Way" in Native American culture in his "'The Harmony Way': Integrating Indigenous Values within Native North American Theology and Mission" (PhD diss., Asbury Theological Seminary, 2010). Randy Woodley often uses the term *Creator* without the definite article ("the Creator") to emphasize God's ongoing gracious activity in creating and sustaining the universe. To describe God as "Creator" expresses a more direct relation to God. Where we are able, we use Woodley's language of "Creator" without the definite article throughout the rest of this book.

[15]Interview with Randy Woodley, American Academy of Religion annual conference, San Francisco, California, November 19, 2012; see Woodley, *Shalom and the Community of Creation.*

[16]See Joerg Rieger, *No Rising Tide: Theology, Economics & the Future* (Minneapolis: Fortress, 2009).

[17]Interview with Darby Ray, American Academy of Religion annual conference, San Francisco, California, November 19, 2012.

Chapter 3: Our Starting Place, the Call of the Poor

[1]Ernesto Cardenal, *The Gospel in Solentiname* (Maryknoll, NY: Orbis, 1976).

[2]For the etymology of *basileia tou theou* see Gerhard Kittel, ed. *Theological Dictionary of the New Testament*, vol. 1 (Grand Rapids: Eerdmans, 1969), pp. 564-93. For recent treatments of Jesus' teaching of the kingdom of God in empire-critical studies see John Dominic Crossan, *God and Empire: Jesus Against Rome, Then and Now* (San Francisco: HarperSanFrancisco, 2007); Obery M. Hendricks Jr., *The Politics of Jesus: Rediscovering the True Revolutionary Nature of the Teachings of Jesus and How They Have Been Corrupted* (New York: Doubleday, 2006); Richard A. Horsley, *Jesus and Empire: The Kingdom of God and the New World Disorder* (Minneapolis: Fortress, 2003). Ada Maria Isasi-Diaz uses the term *kindom*, emphasizing the "kinship" of all creation and the promise of a just future. See Ada Maria Isasi-Diaz, *Mujerista Theology: A Theology for the Twenty-first Century* (Maryknoll, NY: Orbis, 1996), p. 103 n. 8.

[3]Virgilio Elizondo, *Galilean Journey: A Mexican-American Promise* (Maryknoll, NY: Orbis, 1983), pp. 53ff. Obery M. Hendricks Jr., "Galileans: Twice Marginalized," *The Universe Bends Toward Justice: Radical Reflections on the Bible, the Church, and the Body Politic* (Maryknoll, NY: Orbis, 2011), pp. 68-71. Cf. Richard A. Horsley, *Galilee: History, Politics, People* (Valley Forge: Trinity Press International, 1995); Gerd Theissen, *The Shadow of the Galilean* (Philadelphia: Fortress, 1987).

[4]Hendricks, *Politics of Jesus*, pp. 19-23.

[5]Hendricks, *Universe Bends Toward Justice*, p. 123.

[6]Ibid., pp. 52-55.

[7]See Hendricks's interpretation of this exorcism in *Politics of Jesus*, pp. 145-48.

[8]Josephus *The Wars of the Jews* 6.5.3.

[9]Hendricks, *Universe Bends Towards Justice*, pp. 62-67.

[10]By comparison, in Japan the average CEO earns ten times more than the company's lowest-paid workers.

[11]Interview with Rev. Phillip Lawson, Oakland, California, July 2008.

[12]Ibid.

[13]Interview with Joerg Rieger, American Academy of Religion annual conference, San Francisco, California, November 19, 2012.

[14]Che Guevara, *From Algiers to Marcha: The Cuban Revolution Today*, March 12, 1965.

[15]For the history of the Kensington Welfare Rights Union and the poor-led movement for justice they built in Philadelphia, see David Zucchino, *Myth of the Welfare Queen* (New York: Scribner, 1997).

[16]The concept of *kairos* is discussed in more detail in chapter four.

[17]Interview with Liz Theoharis at the Poverty Initiative at Union Theological Seminary, February 25, 2013. Willie Baptist had served as educational director of the Kensington Welfare Rights Union and the co-coordinator of the University of the Poor, the educational arm of the Poor Peoples Economic Human Rights Campaign, established in October 1999. For more of the vision and history of the Poverty Initiative at Union Theological Seminary, see The Poverty Initiative of Union Theological Seminary, *A New and Unsettling Force: Reigniting Rev. Dr. Martin Luther King, Jr.'s Poor People's Campaign* (New York: The Poverty Initiative, 2009); Willie Baptist and Jan Rehman. *Pedagogy of the Poor: Building the Movement to End Poverty* (New York: Teachers College Press, 2011).

[18]With radical roots going back to the 1965 Watts riots in Los Angeles, Willie Baptist has been the elder of the Poverty Initiative, serving as its scholar-in-residence since its founding.

[19]Shane Claiborne, *The Irresistible Revolution: Living as an Ordinary Radical* (Grand Rapids: Zondervan, 2006), p. 65. For the story of the origins of the Simple Way in the St. Ed's takeover see chapter two, pp. 53-68.

[20]Rutba House, ed., *School(s) for Conversion: 12 Marks of the New Monasticism* (Eugene, OR: Wipf & Stock, 2005); Shane Claiborne, Jonathan Wilson-Hartgrove and Enuma Okoro, eds., *Common Prayer: A Liturgy for Ordinary Radicals* (Grand Rapids: Zondervan, 2010).

[21]See "Coalition of Immokalee Workers," in Poverty Initiative, *New and Unsettling Force*, pp. 88-91.

[22]Phone interview with Shane Claiborne, March 2, 2013.

Chapter 4: Discerning the *Kairos*

[1]Interview with Charlie Sherrod, Mobile, Alabama, July 2008.

[2]Interview with Rabbi Leonard Beerman, Los Angeles, California, July 2008.

[3]William Connolly, "The Evangelical-Capitalist Resonance Machine," *Political Theory* 33, no. 6 (December 2005): 874.

[4]William Connolly, *Capitalism and Christianity, American Style* (Durham, NC: Duke University Press, 2008), p. 4.

[5]Ibid., p. 8.

[6]Ibid., p. 36.

[7]Fannie Lou Hamer, quoted in Kay Mills, *This Little Light of Mine: The Life of Fannie Lou Hamer* (Lexington: University Press of Kentucky, 2007), p. 65.

[8]Lynne Olson, "She Kept Daring Us to Go Further," in *Freedom's Daughters: The Unsung Heroines of the Civil Rights Movement from 1830 to 1970* (New York: Scribner, 2001), p. 133; cf. Barbara Ransby, *Ella Baker and the Black Freedom Movement: A Radical Democratic Vision* (Chapel Hill: University of North Carolina Press, 2003).

[9]Olson, *Freedom's Daughters*, p. 139. For a discussion of gender justice in the U.S. civil rights movement with reference to Martin Luther King Jr., see Peter Goodwin Heltzel, *Resurrection City: A Theology of Improvisation* (Grand Rapids: Eerdmans, 2012), pp. 114-21.

[10]Ella Baker, quoted in Vicki L. Crawford, Jacqueline Anne Rouse and Barbara Woods, eds., *Women in the Civil Rights Movement* (Bloomington: Indiana University Press, 1993), p. 51.

Chapter 5: Questions of Power and Hope

[1]I heard this story from Jim Wallis, founder of Sojourners, who witnessed it firsthand. I've since been told by a white South African pastor that Bishop Tutu regularly reached out to enemies and opponents in this way.

[2]Interview with Charlie Sherrod, Mobile, Alabama, July 2008.

[3]Interview with Dolores Huerta, Los Angeles, California, July 2008.

[4]Interview with Darby Ray, American Academy of Religion annual conference, San Francisco, California, November 19, 2012.

[5]Frederick Douglass, "West India Emancipation" speech, Canandaigua, New York, August 3, 1857.

[6]Interview with Nelson and Joyce Johnson, Greensboro, North Carolina, August 2008.

[7]Ibid.

[8]Interview with Cory Beals, American Academy of Religion annual conference, San Francisco, California, November 19, 2012.

[9]Jono Schaefer, clergy meeting, South Los Angeles, California, May 2006.

Chapter 6: The Gift of Christ-Centered Community

[1]This quotation comes from a Latin American representative from the World Council of Churches, speaking at a meeting convened by the Vespers Society, Oakland, California, 1998.

[2]Interview with Darby Ray, American Academy of Religion annual conference, San Francisco, California, November 19, 2012.

[3]Saul Alinsky, *Rules for Radicals* (New York: Vintage, 1989), p. 65.

[4]See Paul Gilroy, *The Black Atlantic: Modernity and Double Consciousness* (Cambridge, MA: Harvard University Press, 1993), esp. pp. 1-40, 72-110. Alan Lomax has demonstrated the Senegalese influence on American slave songs through recordings that intercut Senegalese and Mississippi singers on "African and American Field Songs," on the LP *Roots of the Blues* (New York: New World Records 252, 1977); Georges Niangoran-Boiuah introduces the concept of "the talking drum" as a way to describe the power of African rhythm in mediating the sacred in "The Talking Drum: A Traditional Instrument of Liturgy and of Mediation with the Sacred," in *African Traditional Religions in Contemporary Society,* ed. Jacob K. Olupona (New York: Paragon House, 1991), pp. 81-92.

[5]The metaphor of a deep river is an allusion to the spiritual "Deep River." This song was a powerful symbol in the African American cultural experience, as witnessed in the writings of Langston Hughes, Howard Thurman and James H. Cone. See Langston Hughes, *The Negro Speaks of Rivers* (New York: Disney Jump at the Sun Books, 2009); Howard Thurman, *Deep River: The Negro Spiritual Speaks of Life and Death* (Richmond, IN: Friends United Press, 1975); James H. Cone, *The Spirituals and the Blues: An Interpretation* (Maryknoll, NY: Orbis, 1991).

[6]Jennifer M. McBride, interview at American Academy of Religion annual meeting, San Francisco, November 19, 2012. For a thoughtful treatment of Bonhoeffer's theology for the church's public witness today, see Jennifer M. McBride, *The Church for the World* (Oxford: Oxford University Press, 2012).

[7]Dietrich Bonhoeffer, *Letters and Papers from Prison*, trans. Reginald Fuller et al. (New York: Touchstone, 1997), pp. 281, 286. For a discussion of the *disciplina arcani* in the life and theology of Dietrich Bonhoeffer, see Eberhard Bethge, *Dietrich Bonhoeffer: A Biography*, ed. Victoria Barnett, trans. Eric Mosbacher et al. (Minneapolis: Augsburg Fortress, 2000), pp. 880-84.

[8]For example, the Institute for the Study and Eradication of Jewish Influence on German Church Life, founded in 1939, sought to sever the German Church from Judaism and consolidate German nationalism. While theologians like Karl Barth and Dietrich Bonhoeffer and others in the Confessing Church movement resisted the Nazi regime, most of the Christian leaders

in Germany betrayed Christianity's prophetic ideals and stood by silently as the Nazi propaganda machine put forth the notion of an Aryan Jesus. Robert P. Ericksen and Susannah Heschel, eds., *Betrayal: German Churches and the Holocaust* (Minneapolis: Fortress, 1999); Susannah Heschel, *The Aryan Jesus: Christian Theologians and the Bible in Nazi Germany* (Princeton, NJ: Princeton University Press, 2008); Susannah Heschel, "Transforming Jesus from Jew to Aryan: Protestant Theologians in Nazi Germany," Albert T. Billgray Lecture, University of Arizona, 1995.

Jennifer M. McBride argues that Bonhoeffer's conception of the arcane discipline is relevant for public witness when the church confesses its social sin and repents of it through activist ministries of justice. In contrast to Charles Marsh's interpretation of an arcane discipline that is deeply skeptical of Christian discourse in the public square, McBride argues that there is an important evangelistic role for Christian speech—especially the language of confession, which can be an intelligible and liberating witness to Jesus Christ in a pluralistic society. While the church confesses sin in its liturgical life together, sometimes on the battlefield for justice someone may ask the Christian: "Why are you involved in the movement for justice?" McBride sees this as an opportunity for non-triumphalist confession: confessing the social sin which the faith-rooted organizing is seeking to dismantle, while also confessing Jesus Christ's solidarity with the suffering as the hope of the world. See McBride, *Church for the World,* pp. 51-54.

[9]Charles Marsh, *Wayward Christian Soldiers* (Oxford: Oxford University Press, 2007), p. 148.

[10]Ibid.

[11]Dietrich Bonhoeffer, *Discipleship,* trans. Barbara Green and Reinhard Krauss, vol. 4 of *Dietrich Bonhoeffer Works* (Minneapolis: Fortress, 2003), pp. 110-14.

[12]As quoted by Charles Marsh and John Perkins, *Welcoming Justice: God's Movement Toward Beloved Community* (Downers Grove, IL: InterVarsity Press, 2009), p. 101.

[13]Interview with Randy Woodley, American Academy of Religion annual conference, San Francisco, California, November 19, 2012.

Chapter 7: Individual Gifts

[1]James Flanigan, "Costco Sees Value in Higher Pay," *Los Angeles Times,* February 15, 2004, http://articles.latimes.com/2004/feb/15/business/fi-flan15. Senegal chose to give himself a salary and bonus that equaled only about

twice that of one of his store managers. In 2003 he made $350,000 and declined a bonus, earning him a reputation as one of BusinessWeek 's "Best Managers" in 2003.

[2]Karl Barth, *Der Römerbrief*, p. 390; as quoted in Timothy J. Gorringe, *Karl Barth: Against Hegemony*, 1st ed. (Oxford: Oxford University Press, 1985), p. 46.

[3]Karl Barth, "A Concluding Unscientific Postscript on Schleiermacher," in *The Theology of Schleiermacher*, ed. D. Ritschl, trans. G. W. Bromiley (Grand Rapids: Eerdmans, 1982), p. 264.

[4]Dietrich Bonhoeffer, *Life Together* (San Francisco: HarperOne, 2009).

[5]Parker Palmer, "Prelude," in *Healing the Heart of Democracy* (San Francisco: Jossey-Bass, 2011).

[6]See Martin Buber, "Healing Through Meeting," in *Martin Buber on Psychology and Psychotherapy*, ed. Judith Buber Agassi (Syracuse, NY: Syracuse University Press, 1999), p. 20.

[7]Martin Buber, *I and Thou*, trans. Ronald G. Smith (New York: Charles Scribner's Sons, 1958), p. 135.

Chapter 8: Prophetic Advocacy and Public Witness

[1]John Augustine Ryan, *A Living Wage: Its Ethical and Economic Aspects* (New York: Macmillan, 1906).

[2]Catherine Malabou, *What Should We Do with Our Brain?* trans. Sebastian Rand (New York: Fordham University Press, 2008).

[3]Clayton Crockett and Jeffrey Robbins, *Religion, Politics, and the Earth: The New Materialism* (New York: Palgrave Macmillan, 2012), p. 67.

[4]Hans-Georg Gadamer, *Truth and Method*, 2nd rev. ed., trans. Joel Weinsheimer and Donald G. Marshall (New York: Continuum, 1996), p. 99. Italics are Gadamer's. We are indebted to Bruce Ellis Benson for this quote.

[5]Important works on improvisation include Bruce Ellis Benson's *The Improvisation of Musical Dialogue* (Cambridge: Cambridge University Press, 2005); Samuel Wells, *Improvisation: The Drama of Christian Ethics* (Grand Rapids: Brazos, 2004). See also Peter Goodwin Heltzel, *Resurrection City: A Theology of Improvisation* (Grand Rapids: Eerdmans, 2012).

[6]See Peter Goodwin Heltzel, "Festival Time: The Cadence of the Church as a Musical Theater of the Oppressed," in *Resurrection City: A Theology of Improvisation* (Grand Rapids: Eerdmans, 2012), pp. 130-33.

[7]William T. Cavanaugh *Theopolitical Imagination* (New York: T & T Clark, 2002), p. 98.

[8]Ray Rivera, *Liberating the Captives* (Grand Rapids: Eerdmans, 2012), esp. pp. 80, 99-100.

[9]Interview with Alexie Torres-Fleming, Micah Institute at New York Theological Seminary, April 16, 2013.

[10]For theological reflection on the healing of the land from a Native American evangelical perspective, see Randy Woodley, *Shalom and the Community of Creation* (Grand Rapids: Eerdmans, 2012), pp. 20, 40, 88-90, 102, 126-28.

[11]Jon Sobrino, *Jesus the Liberator: A Historical-Theological Reading of Jesus of Nazareth* (Maryknoll, NY: Orbis, 1993), p. 264.

Chapter 9: Recruitment

[1]Randy Woodley, *Shalom and the Community of Creation* (Grand Rapids: Eerdmans, 2012).

[2]Interview with Charlie Sherrod, Mobile, Alabama, July 2008.

[3]Aryeh Cohen, "Hearing the Cry of the Poor," in *Crisis, Call and Leadership in the Abrahamic Traditions.* ed. Peter Ochs and William Stacy Johnson (New York: Palgrave Macillian, 2009), p. 111.

[4]Peter Ochs, "Philosophic Warrants for Scriptural Reasoning," in *The Promise of Scriptural Reasoning,* ed. David F. Ford and C. C. Pecknold (Malden, MA: Wiley-Blackwell, 2006), p. 130.

[5]Interview with John Fife.

[6]Interview with Rabbi Leonard Beerman, Los Angeles, California, July 2008.

[7]Frederick Buechner, *Wishful Thinking* (San Francisco: HarperOne, 1993), p. 95.

Chapter 10: Developing the Body of Christ

[1]Saul Alinsky, *Rules for Radicals* (New York: Vintage, 1989), p. 74.

[2]Myles Horton, *Long Haul* (New York: Teachers College Press, 1997), p. 35.

[3]Ibid., p. 36.

[4]Ibid., p. 43.

[5]Ibid., p. 62.

[6]Rosa Parks, "Highlander: A Road to Hope," Kentucky Women in the Civil Rights Era, posted April 20, 2011 (www.kywcrh.org/archives/2325).

[7]Horton, *Long Haul.*

[8]Ibid., p. 44.

[9]Paulo Freire, *Pedagogy of the Oppressed* (New York: Bloomsbury Academic, 2000), p. 82.

[10]Martin Luther King Jr., *Where Do We Go from Here?* (Boston: Beacon, 2000).

[11]Gustavo Gutierrez, address to Elmhurst College, Elmhurst, Illinois, September 20, 2009.

[12]Interview with Rabbi Leonard Beerman, Los Angeles, California, July 2008.

[13]Interview with Charlie Sherrod, Mobile, Alabama, July 2008.

[14]Interview with Dolores Huerta, Los Angeles, California, July 2008.

[15]Ibid.

Chapter 11: Prophetic Spirituality

[1]Bob Ekblad, *Reading the Bible with the Damned* (Louisville, KY: Westminster John Knox, 2005).

[2]Interview with Charlie Sherrod, Mobile, Alabama, July 2008.

[3]Ibid.

[4]Martin Luther King Jr., "On the Importance of Jazz," http://wclk.com/dr-martin-luther-king-jr-importance-jazz.

[5]On the singing self, see David Ford, *Self and Salvation* (Cambridge: Cambridge University Press, 1999), pp. 109, 120-29, 235.

[6]See Peter Heltzel, "The Church as a Theatre of the Oppressed," in *Resurrection City* (Grand Rapids: Eerdmans, 2012), chap. 6.

[7]Interview with Dolores Huerta, Los Angeles, California, July 2008.

Index of Names and Subjects